ANCIENT PATHS

DESTINY IMAGE BOOKS BY COREY RUSSELL

The Glory Within: The Interior Life and the Power of Speaking in Tongues

ANCIENT PATHS

REDISCOVERING DELIGHT
IN THE WORD OF GOD

COREY RUSSELL

DESTINY IMAGE® PUBLISHERS, INC.
P.O. Box 310, Shippensburg, PA 17257-0310
"Promoting Inspired Lives."

This book and all other Destiny Image, Revival Press, MercyPlace, Fresh Bread, Destiny Image Fiction, and Treasure House books are available at Christian bookstores and distributors worldwide.

For a U.S. bookstore nearest you, call 1-800-722-6774.
For more information on foreign distributors, call 717-532-3040.
Reach us on the Internet: www.destinyimage.com.

ISBN 13 TP: 978-0-7684-4195-6
ISBN 13 Ebook: 978-0-7684-8754-1

For Worldwide Distribution, Printed in the U.S.A.
1 2 3 4 5 6 7 8 / 16 15 14 13 12

ACKNOWLEDGMENTS

Daniel Paravisini: I want to thank you for running with me and getting down everything the Lord is releasing. I couldn't have done this without you. You have been a true "Baruch" to me.

Jane Harris: You are amazing. Your faithful diligence, servant heart, glad spirit, and ability to labor with me to bring forth this material is truly amazing. Thank you for everything.

ENDORSEMENTS

I believe, without question, that the greatest need in this hour is the knowledge of God imparted into us through times of long and loving meditation in the Word. Corey Russell, in this book, awakens us to the hour we are living in, and then with profound clarity and authority equips us with a vision and tools to go deep in the Word of God. Corey is a faithful man of prayer and the Word, and this book comes out of countless hours in God's presence. It is a must for those who want to go deeper in God.

MIKE BICKLE
Pastor at International House of Prayer, Kansas City
Author of *Passion for Jesus* and *Growing in the Prophetic*

The greatest necessity of the human heart is the ability to hear God. This is the foundation of personal transformation and corporate revival. Throughout redemptive history, God has sent His messengers to call for a return to the precepts of the Word, a return to hearing—illuminating the way to experience abundant life in the Scriptures. Corey Russell's wisdom and practical insight flow from a life rooted in meditation, and his message concerning the need for fresh encounter in the Word of God has never been more relevant than it is today.

ALLEN HOOD
Associate Director, International House of Prayer,
Kansas City;
President of International House of Prayer University

Rarely have I read a book that I feel is so prophetically relevant. *Ancient Paths: Rediscovering Delight in the Word of God* is a clarion call back to the Word of God, to the Word who is God. Those who know their God, as He has revealed Himself through His Word, will emerge as the leaders and the lights in the hour of crisis our world is facing. I strongly urge everyone to read this book.

STACEY CAMPBELL
Author of *Payers of the Bible*

For those longing for a deeper life in the Word of God, Corey Russell offers one of the most passionate, comprehensive, and practical treatises in contemporary Christian literature on spiritually engaging Scripture. In an age when hearing God's Word is all but lost, Mr. Russell systematically challenges us to face this crisis on a personal level. In doing so, he confronts our excuses and lethargy while at the same time exhorting us to join him on the humbling spiritual journey to find Jesus Christ in the pages of holy canon. This is a must read.

CHARLES A. METTEER, PH.D.
Associate Director, Forerunner School of Ministry
International House of Prayer University

CONTENTS

FOREWORD

The very first verse that Corey Russell highlights in this book is Jeremiah 6:10, and God's pain over not being able to speak to anyone because their ears are uncircumcised. I can so identify with Jeremiah and his generation as I feel an even greater crisis mounting in the nations, and my own inability to connect and hear Him like I want. I'm finding myself crying out to God like never before to hear, to perceive, and to connect with His heart. This longing has grown over decades, and has expressed itself in many ways (lots of broken cisterns, see Jer. 2:13), but the longer I'm on this journey, the more I'm realizing how simple, and yet profound the answer is. It sounds so cliché, but the answer to our plight of deafness and my own gnawing pain to hear Him and to discern the hour correctly has been boiled down to one thing: long and loving meditation on the Word of God.

Nothing has changed my life like taking my Bible, closing my eyes, and singing and speaking those phrases back to God. Those words have changed me, convicted me, confronted me, resisted me, washed me, cleansed me, freed me, empowered me, delivered me, and have set me on a course for the rest of my life. When

God's words get in my mouth and I speak those words over my heart, I'm changed. It's bit-by-bit, day-by-day, but I wake up 15 years later and begin to realize that I'm a different person.

This is not a new discovery, but has been the consistent cry and experience of all of God's friends throughout history. We are hearing so much in our day of the "new move" that will shake nations and bring in the revival (and I want it!), but I'm truly coming to the conclusion that the only way forward for our generation is to go back, to go way back, and rediscover how our fathers of the faith found Him, and live accordingly in this hour. The title of this book, *Ancient Paths*, encapsulates this reality better than any phrase or verse I can think of.

I've known and run alongside Corey Russell and his family at IHOP-KC for the last 12 years, and in that time I've witnessed a man who embodies the pages of this book. He is a man who's gripped with the urgency of the hour, and gripped even more with a love affair with the Word of God. He has found a place of true joy, delight, and fascination in the Word, and after reading through this book, I'm convinced that the very passion that he has will be imparted to you as you read it. Not only does he stir up within you a passion for the Word, but he also gives so many profound, practical ways to meditate and to connect with God through the Word. Corey has such an ability to equip this generation in the deeper life, and, without question, this book is a must if you seek to go there.

Misty Edwards

Chapter 1

ANCIENT PATHS

THE PROPHETIC CRISIS

At the beginning of human history, in the Garden of Eden, God made it clear: Eat from this tree and you live; eat from that tree and you will die (see Gen. 2:15-17). His words to Adam and Eve were not suggestions or ideas; they were the difference between life and death. When God called Abram to leave his father's house, his response determined whether or not he would experience eternal separation from God. His life was dependent on his response to the call of God (see Gen. 12:1-3). In the wilderness, God made it clear to the children of Israel that the only way to inherit the promises given to their forefather Abraham was through learning to live by every word that came from the mouth of God (see Deut. 8:3). The Word of God isn't casual and it isn't an option. It is everything.

> *To whom shall I speak and give warning, that they may hear? Indeed their ear is uncircumcised, and they cannot give heed. Behold, the word of the Lord is a reproach to them; they have no delight in it* (Jeremiah 6:10).

God has always been looking for those to whom He can speak, those who will hear Him and live. When Jeremiah wrote these words, Jerusalem was on the brink of destruction. The Babylonian invasion was around the corner, yet the people of the day were blind to their peril. A century earlier the northern tribes of Israel were defeated and dispersed in a season of judgment, but Judah was miraculously spared.[1] Because of this previous divine intervention, the people were convinced that God would spare them again. They were confident in their nationalistic pride while the religious leaders of the day bolstered their confidence further by declaring that God would defend His Temple.

In this context, God went on a search throughout the nation, looking for someone He could speak to and who could speak for Him. God visited and apprehended Jeremiah with a message that was completely different from his contemporaries. This young man from nowhere boldly stated that the people must tremble and rend their hearts. He warned them not to misinterpret the season and mistake God's mercy for indifference. God wasn't overlooking their sin; He was asking them one final time to honestly confront their sin. If they did not, an army was coming from the north as an agent of divine discipline.

The prophet Jeremiah highlighted the crisis of the hour (see Jer. 6:10). He told the people that their inability to hear God and correctly interpret the season was due to the fact that they did not delight in His word. Though they assented to the spiritual laws and reforms being implemented by their leaders, in their hearts they really did not want to hear what God had to say. There was a lack of the word of the Lord in the land. It is interesting to realize that out of all the things Jeremiah could have emphasized in the hour of crisis, he emphasized the people's lack of delight in the prophetic word of the Lord. They did not love God's word, they had not learned to recognize His speech, and they were not vulnerable and tender in their response to Him. In fact, the word of the Lord had been completely forgotten and lost. That was the greatest crisis of Jeremiah's day, and I am convinced it is the crisis of our day as well.

THE CRISIS TODAY

The book you are holding in your hands is not primarily about giving you tools to make your quiet times more bearable. It is about the rediscovery of hearing, delighting in, trembling before, and obeying the Word of God. It is a matter of life and death. I believe we are living in days similar to those described in 1 Samuel 3:1, where it says *"the word of the Lord was rare in those days; there was no widespread revelation."* In that context God raised up a young boy who heard His voice. The Bible says that God *"let none of his* [Samuel's] *words fall to the ground"* (1 Sam. 3:19b). Years ago the Lord spoke to me in a prophetic encounter and said that He was about to rip the feeding tube out of the mouth of the church and teach us how to eat His Word. I believe the current political turmoil and economic shaking in our nation is part of this process. Though it is clear what we are experiencing now is only the beginning of a much greater crisis, the government and the church continue to assert that we should maintain business as usual, and that peace and prosperity are right around the corner.

What many fail to realize is that the last decades of the 20th century—a period in our nation marked by a booming economy and a comparatively peaceful political landscape—produced a new generation of believers who find themselves unequipped for the current crisis. The church today is filled with people who are spiritually starving while "stuffed" with every physical comfort. We have fattened bodies and famished souls. Our hearts are dry, broken, defeated, and deteriorating. Many of our marriages are in shambles. Our children are addicted to video games, movies, and entertainment, and they have no desire for God. Our lives are consumed by the demands of work and the need to pay for the stuff we have accumulated. We have neglected our calling and failed to respond to the simplicity of God's word: Do this and live. Do that and die.

The crisis of our day is the product of many factors, but the one I want to highlight throughout this book is the loss of intimate communion with the Word of God. This fundamental breakdown within the church has now permeated society, and as a result the Word is no longer held as the absolute truth. We, as a people, have not come underneath the Word and have asserted our own ideas, opinions, and desires above God. The question Pilate asked Jesus 2,000 years ago has become the question of the hour: *"What is truth?"* (John 18:38). The belief that God's Word is true and provides the absolute standard of righteousness and morality is no longer widely held. Truth has become a matter of individual ideology and preference, subject only to political correctness. And those of us in the church who continue to affirm the truth of the Word often fail to exhibit that truth in our lives. We preach truth without conforming to it; our values, thoughts, and actions have not been changed and transformed by what we preach. Therefore the power of Scripture is being undermined in our own lives due to our ability to speak the truth without living it. Art Katz describes this phenomenon in his book, *The Spirit of Truth*:

> It would be a grave mistake to think that quoting scriptures correctly or subscribing to the right doctrines wholly constitutes walking in truth. A man may be saying all the right words, yet be contradicting his words by the insincere manner in which he says them. You hear him, and while your intellect is saying "true," your spirit is saying "false." It is possible to know the truth yet not walk in it, and the truth is really in us, and we in it, only to the degree that we actually walk in it.[2]

This is not only a secular and personal crisis; it is also an ecclesiastical and pastoral crisis. In many denominations, truths that have been upheld for centuries by faithful believers are being questioned and the Word of God is being twisted to fulfill human desires. This trend is evident in many of our nation's seminaries, which have become a primary battleground in the war against the authority and truth of Scripture.

The place that is meant to prepare the next generation of leaders is in many places stripping them of their faith and sending them out with stuffed minds and atheistic hearts. A good friend of mine likes to say, "We are living in a day and age where people are confused [about] the deity of Christ but completely clear on the ordination of homosexuals."[3] During his years at school, he was taught that the Bible was merely a history of man's attempt to understand God, a document that contained kernels of truth; but it was not absolute truth. Increasingly, in academic and clerical circles, the Bible is being forced to bend to human desires and individual lifestyle choices. The secularization of our culture is creeping into the church at ever-increasing rates.

Due to the loss of delight in the Word of God, we as the church have invented new ways to capture people's attention. We have replaced the power of the Word with a convenience driven, seeker-friendly church culture. Don't get me wrong—I enjoy a quick Sunday service that lets me out early so I can spend more time with my family. But the truth is that there are many believers who have little heart-connection with the Lord. The entirety of their religious life is relegated to a 45-minute service once a week, while they spend the other 6 days, 23 hours, and 15 minutes of the week tragically disconnected from the life of the Holy Spirit and the power of God's Word.

At its core, this 45-minute expression of Christianity worships the god of convenience. Again, I like convenience—I like wireless Internet, I like good coffee, I like drive-through meals—but when the culture and mentality of convenience seeps into the church it produces selfish, lazy believers. Congregations live vicariously off of the man or woman in the pulpit, and individuals no longer feel personally responsible for deepening their relationship with God and growing in their knowledge of His Word. Sadly, the same realities are true among the shepherds. Many of us in leadership have spent more energy and resources on the expansion of our spheres of influence than on the expansion of our hearts.

The crisis related to the Word of God has touched the core of our hearts. The culture of convenience has produced a generation that is enslaved to instant gratification and to comfort: we refuse to invest in anything that costs us time and energy. Our souls are addicted to the things of the world, and because of this the chaos and traffic of the culture has permeated our internal lives. Materialism has drowned and crowded out the still, small voice. Our hearts are surrounded on every side with images, voices, and busyness that have choked the Word in our hearts. Jesus said, *"Now he who received seed among the thorns is he who hears the word, and the cares of this world and the deceitfulness of riches choke the word, and he becomes unfruitful"* (Matt. 13:22). As a result, we have lost the ability to hear and the simplicity of delighting in the Word of God.

Faith rests on our ability to hear God's Word (see Rom. 10:17). As we lose our ability to hear, we begin to fall into unbelief. Stephen Charnock coined the phrase "practical atheism" to describe believers who verbally assent to the existence of God but whose hearts have ceased to love, believe, and follow Him.[4] In Psalm 14:1, the psalmist declares, *"The fool has said in his heart, 'There is no God.'"* Notice that the fool doesn't say it in front of other people. Rather, he says it in his heart—by the way he lives, by what he does with his time and his money. He may outwardly confess God, but inwardly he is an atheist. This is, in my opinion, the primary reason for the absence of living faith in our lives, our families, and our expression in the earth as the body of Christ. We may have all the facts and statistics down, but the power of Christianity is found when the information makes the journey from the mind to the heart. The ultimate aim is the impact on our hearts, which then transforms what we do with our time, money, and energy. The Word is meant to abide in us and transform us from the inside out.

THE SOLUTION TO THE CRISIS

Hans Urs von Balthasar[5] says in his wonderful book on prayer,

> Harassed by life, exhausted, we look about us for somewhere to be quiet, to be genuine, a place of refreshment. We yearn to restore our spirits in God, to simply let go in him and gain new strength to go on living. But we fail to look for him where he is waiting for us, where he is to be found: in his Son, who is his Word. Or else we seek for God because there are a thousand things we want to ask him, and imagine that we cannot go on living unless they are answered. We inundate him with problems, with demands for information, for clues, for an easier path, forgetting that in his Word he has given us the solution to every problem and all the details we are capable of grasping in this life. We fail to listen where God speaks: where God's Word rang out in the world once for all, sufficient for all ages, inexhaustible. Or else we think that God's word has been heard on earth for so long that by now it is almost used up, that it is about time for some new word, as if we had the right to demand one. We fail to see that it is we ourselves who are used up and alienated, whereas the word resounds with the same vitality and freshness as ever; it is just as near to us as

it always was. "The word is near you, on your lips and in your heart" (Rom 10:8).[6]

My desire in this book is to speak to those who, if they are honest with themselves, admit that the Word of God is one of the most frustrating and boring places in the world. I want to take you on a journey from the pain of barrenness into the joy of breakthrough by sharing keys that will unlock the Word of God until it becomes a place of delight, pleasure, fascination, correction, and transformation. The book you are holding is about recovering our love for the Word of God and rediscovering the power of Scripture and its impact on the human soul.

Jeremiah the prophet indicts the people and says that the word of the Lord is not a delight to them (see Jer. 6:10). Then, several verses later, he calls them to the ancient paths:

> *Thus says the Lord: "Stand in the ways and see, and ask for the old paths* [ancient paths, ESV], *where the good way is, and walk in it; then you will find rest for your souls"* (Jeremiah 6:16).

It is clear from the context of this passage that the "ancient paths" refer to the simplicity of delighting in the Word of God. In every hour of crisis, God calls His people back to love of the Word; He calls them to silence the other voices in their lives and cultivate hearing hearts. And though it has been 2,500 years since Jeremiah cried out to his generation, the ancient paths remain the clearest solution to the crisis of our day. The only way forward is to go back. Just as the fathers of our faith sought God through their simple lives, so we too must seek Him. We have lost the inner sanctum, the place of communion where we can hear God, and so we must reclaim the ability to withdraw inwardly and, as A.W. Tozer says, "meet God in adoring silence."[7] Only then will we experience the restoration of our hearts, our lives, and our ministries, and reclaim the ability to rightly discern the hour we are living in.

The question we now face is this: How do we find these ancient paths and return to the place of communion, the place of hearing? The answer is found in Jeremiah 6:16. We are given two clear commands in this verse: stand and ask. Standing places us in a position of active determination. It requires strength to resist the current of the culture and the pull of our own nature. When we stand before God, we cease looking for answers within ourselves. Instead, we begin to turn to Him for answers. We must take the time to stop in the midst of our crowded lives and ask God what these ancient paths look like in our 21st-century Western context. Asking places us in a position of humility before the Lord. It brings us to our knees in prayer and requires us to acknowledge that we will not succeed in our own strength.

If we stand and ask for the ancient paths, the promise is that we will find rest for our souls. The rest described by Jeremiah is not a *siesta* or a break from real life—it is a place of peace in the midst of the storm. True peace is a rare thing. We are surrounded by hundreds of reasons to be anxious. Our lives are driven by the demands of work, finances, and relationships—each more stressful than the next. And when our circumstances are momentarily peaceful, we are faced with the restlessness of our souls. This is why supernatural peace is the greatest need of the hour. When our souls are at rest, we are able to sleep in the stern of the boat though it is tossed by the wind and waves (see Mark 4:35-40). We are able to hear God clearly regardless of the trials and pressures we face. In the midst of personal and national crises, the ability to rest will be our greatest refuge and anchor. This is why it is so critical to seek the ancient paths.

There have been many seasons where the Lord has used Jeremiah 6:16 to call me back to the place of hearing Him. I remember the first time I experienced the desire to retreat from a crowded life, a crowded soul, and a culture that was choking the Word in my own heart. I stumbled upon the Desert Fathers— men (and women) who retreated into the wilderness of Egypt in the third and fourth centuries in order to escape the increasing synchronization of the church and culture. In his book *The Wisdom of the Desert* Thomas Merton describes the belief of these early contemplatives:

> Society...was regarded by them as a shipwreck from which each single individual man had to swim for his life.... These were men who believed that to let oneself drift along, passively accepting the tenets and values of what they knew as society, was purely and simply a disaster.[8]

The parallels between their day and ours struck me: after centuries of persecution, Christianity was finally given political approval and protection by the Roman Emperor Constantine. While this might sound like good news, to the Desert Fathers it was cause for concern. They understood the dangers of integrating faith and culture. They knew that, at its core, Christianity was at war with the ways of the world, and if the external expression of that war was removed, believers would be lulled into a false sense of peace, eventually falling into compromise. As Henri Nouwen states in the introduction to his book on the Desert Fathers, "If the world was no longer the enemy of the Christian, then the Christian had to become the enemy of the dark world. The flight to the desert was the way to escape a tempting conformity to the world."[9] And so these early contemplatives chose to purposefully seek out solitude and silence. They knew that by retreating to the wilderness, their hearts would be prepared to once again hear the Word of God.

When I first read about these men and women, it produced the desire within me to separate myself from the distractions of my own life. I realized that I desperately needed to internally change;

somehow I had to pull away from the tentacles of the culture that had ensnared my heart—the media, the music, the images, and the voices that daily surrounded me. As I learned more about the contemplative lifestyle pursued by the Desert Fathers, I realized that though my context was radically different from theirs, the heart realities produced through long and loving meditation on the Word of God were still available to me. And not only were they available—they were absolutely necessary.

> We are in danger of drowning on the open sea, and God's word is the rope ladder thrown down to us so that we can climb up into the rescuing vessel. It is the carpet, rolled out toward us so that we can walk along it to the Father's throne.[10]

God's Word is His invitation to be with Him where He is. From before the foundation of the world it has been His desire for us to be with Him, to know His heart, to experience His emotions, to be filled with His thoughts, to be transformed into His image, and to live in unity with Him. Beloved, the fulfillment of this desire is found in His Word. We've looked everywhere else—we are dry, tired souls and we don't know where to find true transformation. But God has extended His invitation and the carpet is rolled out. Over and over in the Scriptures we see Him visit the thirsty souls and offer them water that will quench their deepest desires.[11]

Today I believe the Lord is visiting our generation. He is alluring us and wooing us in this season to hear again, to come again, to believe again. The Lord is calling the dry, tired souls back to the place of rest. Jeremiah's words are as alive today as they were thousands of years ago. We want to respond to his cry and begin to ask God for the ancient paths—for the paths of prayer, for the paths of the Word, and for the paths of silence, meditation, and contemplation. It is our desire to rediscover the place of inner quiet where the Word of God can speak. We want to go on the journey of rediscovering the ability to hear.

Chapter 2

JESUS THE WORD

The Word of God is born out of the eternal silence of God, and it is to this Word out of silence that we want to be witnesses. Silence is the home of the word. Silence gives strength and fruitfulness to the word. We can even say that words are meant to disclose the mystery of the silence from which they come.[1]

It was in the silence and stillness that the word of God was first released. In the opening verses of Genesis, we see the Spirit of God brooding over the deep (see Gen. 1:2). The Father's heart is filled with plans, desires, dreams, intentions, and thoughts—all yet to be expressed and manifested. *"The earth was without form, and void; and darkness was on the face of the deep. And the Spirit of God was hovering over the face of the waters"* (Gen. 1:2). We know what happened next, but I want us to stop for a moment, quiet our souls, and gaze on the mystery of the Word. As the Spirit hovered over the deep, waiting and anticipating, the unimaginable happened. The voice of God broke the silence of eternity and filled the void with light and creation.

"Then God said, 'Let there be light'; and there was light" (Gen. 1:3). The God of eternity—the omnipotent, omniscient, omnipresent Creator—chose to speak light into existence. He didn't blink it, think it, or even wish it; instead, He spoke it. In that moment He showed us the nature of His word. God's word is the external expression of His heart; His thoughts, plans, and desires are communicated and realized through His word. *"Let there be light"* caused those things hidden within the Father from before the foundations of the earth to be made manifest. God spoke, and through this word the heavens and the earth were made. It is this word that we are seeking to hear once again.

THE NATURE OF GOD'S WORD

Words are powerful; they reveal the hidden things of the heart. They communicate, describe, create, express, enlighten, and empower. I am amazed many times by the volume of emotion contained in a single phrase. When I look at my wife and say, "I love you," I am expressing a flood of feelings with three simple words. "I love you" actually contains a library of thoughts, memories, and emotions. It takes an intangible feeling, and creates a vehicle for communication and shared experience. This is the power of words in their purest form.

However, we are living in a day where words are steadily being stripped of their power. Nouwen accurately describes this phenomenon:

> Over the last few decades we have been inundated by
> a torrent of words. Wherever we go we are surrounded
> by words: words softly whispered, loudly proclaimed,
> or angrily screamed; words spoken, recited, or sung;
> words on records, in books, on walls, or in the sky;
> words in many sounds, many colors, or many forms;
> words to be heard, read, seen, or glanced at; words

which flicker off and on, move slowly, dance, jump, or wiggle. Words, words, words! They form the floor, the walls, and the ceiling of our existence.

It has not always been this way. There was a time not too long ago without radios and televisions, stop signs, yield signs, merge signs, bumper stickers, and the ever-present announcements indicating price increases or special sales. There was a time without the advertisements which now cover whole cities with words.

Recently I was driving through Los Angeles, and suddenly I had the strange sensation of driving through a huge dictionary. Wherever I looked there were words trying to take my eyes from the road. They said, "Use me, take me, buy me, drink me, smell me, touch me, kiss me, sleep with me." In such a world who can maintain respect for words?

All this is to suggest that words, my own included, have lost their creative power. Their limitless multiplication has made us lose confidence in words and caused us to think, more often than not, "They are just words."[2]

Our words have been devalued through overuse and painful life experiences. In essence, we have learned to distrust words. How many of us have pasts filled with broken promises? Dad said "I love you" with his mouth, but his actions said "I have no time for you." The boyfriend or girlfriend we opened our heart to in high school said "I love you," but they loved someone else within a month. Life has taught us that love is not eternal, that it falls apart quickly when someone or something else comes along, and that it is not what we hoped it was. We are no longer moved by the word *love* because of our experiences connected to that word.

The value of words has been lost. After years of hearing teachers, parents, and authority figures speak at us, we have learned to look engaged while tuning out. We have actually trained ourselves to *not* listen. I believe that rediscovering the ancient paths will require us to leave behind our overfamiliarity with the Bible, along with our tendency to discount the words on the page, so that we may truly feel its weight again. Too often we fail to realize that when God speaks, His words are backed by His nature—and His nature is transcendent and incorruptible.

Jesus said, *"Heaven and earth will pass away, but My words will by no means pass away"* (Matt. 24:35).

THE WORD IN THE OLD TESTAMENT

> Finally, God's word is himself, his most vital, his innermost self: his only-begotten Son, of the same nature as himself, sent into the world to bring it home, back to him. And so God speaks to us from heaven and commends to us his Word, dwelling on earth for a while: "This is my beloved Son: listen to him" (Matt. 17:5).[3]

We cannot talk about the Word of God without talking about the Word who is God. The Word that manifested the Father's heart and plans in Genesis when light first dispelled darkness is the same Word that manifests the Father today. Jesus is the eternal expression of the Father, the embodiment and communication of God. In the beginning was the Word: this Word is God's own Self, this Word is God's own Son (see John 1:1).

Throughout the Old Testament we see Jesus communicating the heart of the Father. In Genesis 1 He articulated the Father's thoughts and plans at creation. The Gospel of John states that Jesus was present before the foundation of the earth (see John 1:2-3), the writer of Hebrews declares that through Jesus the worlds were made (see Heb. 1:2), and Paul states in his letter to the Colossians that all things were created by Him (see Col. 1:16). As the Word, He revealed Himself to the patriarchs, appearing at significant times to lead the nation of Israel in times of crisis. In these encounters He is referred to sometimes as "God Himself," sometimes as "one like the Son of Man," and frequently as the "Angel of the Lord." The title "Angel of the Lord" is specifically used to describe Jesus when He appeared to various individuals before His incarnation. When we examine the accounts of these appearances, we find descriptions of one who appears as a man or angelic being (the Hebrew word for *angel* can also be translated simply as "messenger"), but speaks as God. In his commentary on the book of Zechariah, David Baron sums up the identity of the Angel of the Lord:

> The "man," as we are told in ver. 11, was the Malakh Yehovah—the Angel of Jehovah, who is none other than the "Angel of His face," the Divine "Angel of the Covenant," the second person in the Blessed Trinity, whose early manifestation to the patriarch and prophets, as the "Angel" or Messenger of Jehovah in the form of man, were anticipations of His incarnation and of that incomprehensible humiliation to which He would afterwards condescend for our salvation.[4]

In Genesis 22 the Angel of the Lord spoke with Abraham:

And Abraham stretched out his hand and took the knife to slay his son.

*But **the Angel of the Lord called to him from heaven** and said, "Abraham, Abraham!"*

So he said, "Here I am."

*And He said, "Do not lay your hand on the lad, or do anything to him; for now I know that you fear God, **since you have*** *not withheld your son, your only son, from Me"* (Genesis 22:10-12).

When Jacob wrestled with a Man until morning, he declared he had seen the face of God:

Then Jacob was left alone; and a Man wrestled with him until the breaking of day.... So Jacob called the name of the place Peniel: "For I have seen God face to face, and my life is preserved" (Genesis 32:24,30).

In Exodus, the Angel of the Lord appeared to Moses in the burning bush and commissioned him to deliver the people of Israel:

And the Angel of the Lord appeared to him [Moses] **in a flame of fire from the midst of a bush.** *So he looked, and behold, the bush was burning with fire, but the bush was not consumed.... So when the Lord saw that he turned aside to look,* **God called to him from the midst of the bush and said...***"I am the God of your father—the God of Abraham, the God of Isaac, and the God of Jacob."* *And Moses hid his face, for he was afraid to look upon God* (Exodus 3:2,4,6).

In Joshua 5:13-15, Jesus appeared to Joshua as the Commander of the Army of the Lord. In Judges 6:11-14, the Angel of the Lord visited Gideon and strengthened him to lead the Israelites into battle against their enemies. In his vision of the heavenly temple, Isaiah saw the Son exalted in His glory (see Isa. 6:1-5; John 12:41). In Jeremiah 1:9, Jesus touched the prophet's mouth and commissioned him for ministry. He caused Ezekiel to eat a scroll containing words of judgment and woe for the nations (see Ezek. 2:9-3:2). When Shadrach, Meshach, and Abednego were thrown into the furnace, Jesus was the fourth man in the fire—and Nebuchadnezzar declared that His appearance was as the Son of God (see Dan. 3:24-25). In a night vision, the Angel of the Lord appeared to Zechariah and proclaimed God's zeal for

Jerusalem (see Zech. 1:12-21). Again and again throughout the Old Testament, Jesus communicated the mind, heart, and will of the Father to the nation of Israel as the Word of God.

THE WORD IN THE NEW TESTAMENT

And then there was silence. Malachi was the last prophet of the Old Testament. After his ministry, the nation endured 400 years without receiving any fresh revelation. It was as though Israel had returned to the stillness that preceded the release of God's word at creation. A holy hush fell on the land. Yet as the centuries passed, the people of God never ceased waiting for Him to speak again. Under the oppression of the Roman Empire, the sense of expectation grew: God would not be silent forever. The same Holy Spirit that was brooding over the deep in Genesis was now stirring in the hearts of men and women, awakening faith and a fresh longing for the final Word. In Jerusalem, Simeon clung to the promise given to him by the Spirit that he would not see death before he had seen the Christ (see Luke 2:25-26). In the Temple, Anna gave her life to prayer and fasting as she looked for the redemption of God (see Luke 2:36-38). The Holy Spirit within these intercessors was waiting for the Word to be released. And at the climax of longing and expectation, God spoke:

In the beginning was the Word, and the Word was with God, and the Word was God. He was in the beginning with God. All things were made through Him, and without Him nothing was made that was made. In Him was life, and the life was the light of men. And the light shines in the darkness, and the darkness did not comprehend it....

And the Word became flesh and dwelt among us, and we beheld His glory, the glory as of the only begotten of the Father, full of grace and truth (John 1:1-5,14).

In the fullness of time, God released His ultimate Word. It was the same Word that was with Him in the beginning, the same Word that visited the fathers of the faith and led the people of God. It was the Word that the prophets foretold when they declared, *"Behold, the virgin shall conceive and bear a Son, and shall call His name Immanuel"* (Isa. 7:14), *"which is translated, 'God with us'"* (Matt. 1:23). In Jesus, God spoke to humanity and said, "I will be joined to you forever." The Second Person of the Trinity took on the form of His creation and dwelt among us.

> *God, who at various times and in various ways spoke in time past to the fathers by the prophets, has in these last days spoken to us by His Son, whom He has appointed heir of all things, through whom also He made the worlds; who being the brightness of His glory and the express image of His person, and upholding all things by the word of His power, when He had by Himself purged our sins, sat down at the right hand of the Majesty on high...* (Hebrews 1:1-3).

Everything about the life of Jesus communicated the Father. The humility of His birth, the anonymity of His childhood, the compassion of His ministry, the brutality of His death, and the power of His resurrection—these were transcripts from God's holy heart. In John 17:26, as Jesus prayed to the Father in the final hours before His arrest, He stated, *"I have declared to them Your name."* Everything He did and everything He didn't do, everything He said and everything He didn't say, declared the name and nature of God. He was the exact expression and the manifestation of the Father.

Through Jesus' miracles we hear that God is a Healer. Through His dealings with sinners we encounter the merciful God. Through His parables we discover the God who hides His mysteries in everyday language. When He cursed the fig tree and walked on the waves, we are awed by His sovereignty. In His invitation to the woman at the well, we witness God restoring the emotionally broken. In His clashes with the Pharisees, we feel God's righteous anger toward hypocrisy and injustice. By Jesus' own mouth we learn that God is *"gentle and lowly in heart"* (Matt. 11:29). Through the cleansing of the Temple, we encounter God's zeal in judging sin. And through His death, Jesus shows us the God who holds nothing back in redeeming the people who rejected Him.

Jesus told the disciples in John 14, *"He who has seen Me has seen the Father"* (John 14:9). He brought the revelation of the Father to the world. As we gaze at His life, we realize not only that God is speaking, but that He is speaking in a language we can understand. God came and took on our form: He looked like us, He lived like us, and He spoke like us. Through Jesus, God became touchable.

> *That which was from the beginning, which we have heard, which we have seen with our eyes, which we have looked upon, and our hands have handled, concerning the Word of life—the life was manifested, and we have seen, and bear witness, and declare to you that eternal life which was with the Father and was manifested to us...* (1 John 1:1-2).

His life built the bridge between God and humanity. As we stated earlier, this is the power of words. They build communication and relationship, and they express those things hidden in the heart of the speaker. In His humility, God chose to speak to us on our terms through Jesus. In his letter to the Colossians, Paul states, *"He is the image of the invisible God"* (Col. 1:15a). In other words, we know what God looks like because we have seen His Son. *"No one has seen God at any time. The only begotten Son, who is in the bosom of the Father, He has declared Him"* (John 1:18). God is declared through Christ. Everything about the life of Jesus is God talking to us.

Christ's suffering, his God-forsakenness, his death and descent into hell is the revelation of a divine mystery, the language which God has chosen in order to render himself and his love intelligible to us…. This Word, this language, is Jesus Christ; not merely a selection of his words and deeds, but he himself, whole and entire.[5]

As the Word of God, Jesus declared the name of the Father. He declared it on the cross, saying to the world forever, "This is what God is like." He declared it at the resurrection, breaking the power of death. He declared it at His ascension, taking His rightful place at the Father's side. For the last 2,000 years He has continued to declare the name of God as our eternal intercessor (see Heb. 7:25). And He is going to ultimately declare it at His second coming. When He appears to openly and globally confront and forever destroy sin, death, and Satan, He will be recognized as the Word of God—the final and eternal communication and expression of the Father to humanity.

…and His name is called The Word of God (Revelation 19:13b).

Chapter 3

THE CALL TO HEAR

THE ROAD TO EMMAUS

It is impossible to listen to any individual word of God without hearing the Son who is the Word. Moreover, it is futile to leaf through the writings of the Old and New Covenants in the hope of coming across truths of one kind or another, unless we are prepared to be exposed to a direct encounter with him, with this personal, utterly free Word which makes sovereign claims upon us.[1]

When we begin to understand that the Bible was given to us for the sake of encountering a Person, it transforms the essential way we approach the Word of God. We are no longer interested in reading for information alone; instead, we are awakened to the longing for relationship and dialogue with God. The Father sent His Son to begin a conversation with us and to show us the way back to Himself. Jesus is the ladder, the door, the communication line between heaven and earth. When we encounter this Word, He escorts us into the heart of God.

God desires that we would see the Scriptures as the vehicle through which we meet Jesus, who is the Word. Jesus Himself taught the disciples to find Him in the Word when He journeyed with them on the road to Emmaus.

> *Now behold, two of them were traveling that same day to a village called Emmaus, which was seven miles from Jerusalem. And they talked together of all these things which had happened. So it was, while they conversed and reasoned, that Jesus Himself drew near and went with them. But their eyes were restrained, so that they did not know Him.*
>
> *And He said to them, "What kind of conversation is this that you have with one another as you walk and are sad?"*
>
> *Then the one whose name was Cleopas answered and said to Him, "Are You the only stranger in Jerusalem, and have You not known the things which happened there in these days?"* (Luke 24:13-18)

This is one of the most fascinating stories in the Bible. Cleopas and another disciple were walking on the road to Emmaus shortly after the events of the crucifixion. As they were traveling and talking, Jesus appeared to them, interrupting them in order to ask what their conversation was all about. You can tell from his response that Cleopas was a bold man! He said in essence, "Where have You been? Are You the only one who hasn't heard the news?" look at how Jesus responded: He baits them by feigning ignorance and asks, "What news?"

> *And He* [Jesus] *said to them, "What things?"*
>
> *So they said to Him, "The things concerning Jesus of Nazareth, who was a Prophet mighty in deed and word before God and all the people, and how the chief priests and our rulers*

delivered Him to be condemned to death, and crucified Him. But we were hoping that it was He who was going to redeem Israel. Indeed, besides all this, today is the third day since these things happened. Yes, and certain women of our company, who arrived at the tomb early, astonished us. When they did not find His body, they came saying that they had also seen a vision of angels who said He was alive. And certain of those who were with us went to the tomb and found it just as the women had said; but Him they did not see" (Luke 24:19-24).

Cleopas responded by admitting, "We believed Jesus of Nazareth was the Savior, but He died like every other prophet and now we don't know what to think." The honesty of his answer is exactly what Jesus was looking for. He wanted to expose what was truly in their hearts in order to provoke dialogue and release revelation. Now He had the opportunity to do so, and He is just as bold as Cleopas in His rebuke:

Then He said to them, "O foolish ones, and slow of heart to believe in all that the prophets have spoken! Ought not the Christ to have suffered these things and to enter into His glory?" ***And beginning at Moses and all the Prophets, He expounded to them in all the Scriptures the things concerning Himself*** (Luke 24:25-27).

Beginning in the book of Genesis, Jesus unveiled the storyline of God's redemption. He walked them through the Law and the Prophets, and instructed them concerning the suffering of Christ and His resurrection. The story of Jesus taking on flesh and coming to earth starts with *"In the beginning"* (Gen. 1:1)—and that is where we must start as well. When you read Genesis, Leviticus, or even Ezekiel, do you see Christ throughout the Scriptures? Has Jesus revealed Himself to your heart through the Word? Luke continues:

Then they drew near to the village where they were going, and He indicated that He would have gone farther. But they constrained Him, saying, "Abide with us, for it is toward evening, and the day is far spent." And He went in to stay with them (Luke 24:28-29).

After unpacking the entire Old Testament, Jesus let them decide how they would respond. He was ready to keep walking—they had reached a fork in the road and He said, "I'll see you later"—but the two disciples constrained Him. In other words, they replied, "We don't think so," and grabbed Him.

This is how we should respond when we encounter the Word of God. But when Jesus begins to release revelation to our spirits, most of us do not hold on to Him. We complete our allotted reading time and then move on with our day, never realizing that the kingdom of heaven suffers violence (see Matt. 11:12). Only desperate people who grab God and hold on to Him receive encounter. Jesus wants us to act on our desperation and take the time to be with Him. He is waiting for us to hold Him and say, "Come in and abide with me. Let's eat, let's fellowship, let's take this conversation further." We do not have to be satisfied with only a little revelation. We can receive impartation and be transformed by an encounter with the living Word.

Now it came to pass, as He sat at the table with them, that He took bread, blessed and broke it, and gave it to them. Then their eyes were opened... (Luke 24:30-31a).

After they invited Him to abide with them, Jesus sat at the table, took the bread, blessed it, and broke it. When He did this, their eyes were supernaturally opened to see Him. This means that their eyes were earlier restrained. Although they had the urge to stay in the conversation, they were longing for more. Even though they were receiving revelation, and the power of God was all around them, they had not yet seen Jesus. It was only when He came in and broke bread with them that they knew Him.

> *And they said to one another, "Did not our heart burn within us while He talked with us on the road, and while He opened the Scriptures to us?"* (Luke 24:32)

"Did not our hearts burn within us as He unfolded the Scriptures?" I am convinced that the true purpose of the Word of God is to cause our hearts to burn with love and tenderness toward God. When the Word communicated the Word to their spirits, they felt it. It touched them. It was more than a Bible study. It was an encounter.

Just as He did for the disciples, Jesus wants to take us on the road to Emmaus. He wants to walk us through the Old and New Testaments and reveal who He is in the Scriptures. We were made for more than living on the fringes of all that is available to us; we were made to encounter the Person on the other side of the pages. However, God is waiting for us to lay hold of Him with spiritual violence and say, "Come in and abide with me." Jesus would have kept walking if the disciples had not constrained Him.

There are seasons when He gives us a little revelation and then waits to see what we will do with it. Song of Solomon 3 describes such a season. The bride rises up to search for her beloved, and when she finds him, she declares, *"I held him and would not let him go"* (Song of Sol. 3:4). In Genesis 28 Jacob wrestled with God and would not let Him go without receiving breakthrough. There is a tenacity produced in our hearts through these seasons of spiritual violence. It is only when we hold on to God and enter into the place of abiding that our eyes are truly opened, we leave dead religion, and we enter into encounter.

My desire in writing this book is to help you embark on the journey of a burning heart. The Bible is meant to touch your inner self and set you on fire. When the disciples saw Jesus vanish before their eyes, the only thing they could talk about was how their hearts were burning as He spoke. Their experience of the Word was more powerful than the miracle they witnessed with their eyes! We want this to be our experience as well: we want a heart set on fire, a heart that is tenderized, illuminated, renewed, and inflamed. Our God is an all-consuming fire (see Heb. 12:29). In his vision of Jesus, Ezekiel described Him as the Son of Man with the appearance of fire and amber (see Ezek. 8:2). In Revelation, the apostle John declared that His eyes were flames of fire and His face was like the sun (see Rev. 1:14-16). He is the burning God. Everything around Him is on fire; and if we draw near to Him, we will be set ablaze.

Many of us resist this call to cultivate a burning heart because we have been taught that our faith is not based on feelings. Unfortunately, we have thrown the baby out with the bath water. We cannot be led by our emotions, but we also cannot sustain our faith unless the power of God touches our hearts. What is love if you don't feel it? What is encounter if you don't experience it? The Word was made to touch you and move your emotions. You were made to cry out as Jeremiah did: *"His word was in my heart like a burning fire"* (Jer. 20:9). God wants to write His Word on your heart; He wants you to feel it and delight in it. You were made to encounter Him.

THE CALL TO HEAR

He who has ears to hear, let him hear! (Matthew 11:15)

Six times in the Gospels and eight times in the book of Revelation we are called to hear.[2] In one place Jesus warns us to take heed *how* we hear, and in another He instructs us to take heed *what* we hear (see Luke 8:18; Mark 4:24). Bob Sorge, author of *In His Face*, says that the word *hear* is the most important word in the Bible: "Everything in the gospel is predicated upon truly and simply hearing what God is saying."[3]

But what does it truly mean to hear? On the road to Emmaus, the disciples did not just listen to Jesus expound upon the Scriptures with their natural ears; their spirits were also engaged. The information they received through their natural sense of hearing moved from their minds to their hearts and internally transformed them until they were burning with revelation. This is what Jesus means when He calls us to hear. When we hear, our hearts are awakened and our spiritual senses are opened to revelation. Hearing leads to encounter.

As we highlighted in the first chapter, the core breakdown of Jeremiah's day was the people's inability to hear the prophetic word for their generation. They did not discern the hour they were living in because their hearts and ears were untrained. Not much had changed when Jesus walked the streets of Jerusalem over 500 years after Jeremiah. The same self-righteousness, complacency, and apathy that prevented Jeremiah's generation from hearing the word of God also afflicted Jesus' generation.

In John's Gospel, Jesus indicts the religious leaders because of their refusal to come to Him and hear His words (see John 5:33-42). These men were experts concerning the Word of God and the coming of the Messiah. As Pharisees, they spent many hours each day reading, studying, and meditating on the Torah. That was their job: they spoke the Word of God, they taught the Word of God, and they lived in the atmosphere of the Word of God. But when the Word made flesh showed up in their midst, they were blind to His identity and accused Him of being demonized. What was the cause of their deception? These were sincere men who were called to ministry and desired to give themselves radically to the Word of God, yet somewhere along the way their sincerity became arrogance. The Pharisees believed that they were protecting the people from deception; they began their journey as lovers of truth! Where did they lose their discernment? At what point did they cease to truly hear? How could they fail to recognize truth when He was standing before them?

We are often tempted to view the Pharisees from a distance and make an example of them. But human nature has not changed in the last 2,000 years; and so when Jesus speaks to these men, He is also addressing the Pharisee within you and me. There are places in our hearts where we have hesitated and at times refused to submit to the demands of truth. Take a moment and consider the stories of these men: When they were young they had genuine hunger for God, a deep love for the Scriptures, and a calling to ministry. Over time, however, their humility, purity, and zeal turned to pride, self-righteousness, hypocrisy, and a lack of love. While their minds grew bigger, their hearts grew smaller. They really believed what they were doing was right, but there was a breakdown—they lost discernment because of their approach to the Word of God.

Jesus began to address this breakdown directly when He described the Pharisees' response to the ministry of John the Baptist:

> *You have sent to John, and he has borne witness to the truth. Yet I do not receive testimony from man, but I say these things that you may be saved. He was the burning and shining lamp, and **you were willing** for a time to rejoice in his light* (John 5:33-35).

I want to emphasize the word *willing*. The first barrier to hearing is found in the issue of being willing. John was a turning signal and his ministry was meant to point toward the revelation of Christ. The religious leaders were willing to go and listen to John because journeying into the desert and hearing his message didn't demand a response from them. Jesus said in essence, "It didn't cost you to go to the desert and attend the John the Baptist conference. He was the burning and shining lamp, and you were willing for a time to rejoice in his light. You traveled into the wilderness to watch the burning man burn. You danced and rejoiced, but you missed the point."

Then Jesus shifts the indictment:

You have neither heard His [God's] *voice at any time, nor seen His form. But you do not have His word abiding in you, because whom He sent, Him you do not believe* (John 5:37b-38).

Can you feel the intensity of this statement? Imagine the deafening silence that must have followed it. If there was one thing the Pharisees prided themselves on, it was their knowledge of God. They were surrounded by the Word—it was in their synagogues, their homes, and their very mouths. Yet when the Son of God stood before them, they thought He was a demoniac and a false Messiah. Their inability to believe in Him exposed the fact that the Word did not truly abide in them. The Pharisees were willing to go and hear John the Baptist, but when they came into contact with Jesus, something inside of them was unwilling to bow in humility at the revelation of God. Jesus looked directly at them and declared: "You have never heard God, you have never seen Him, and His Word has no place in your life. It does not abide in you." Take a moment and ask yourself these questions: What does it mean for the Word to abide in you? What does it look like when the Word takes up residence in your interior life?

The Word of God is the fork in the road: it will produce either tenderness or hardness in us based on the posture of our hearts. There is no neutral ground and no room for passivity in our approach to Scripture. The Word is living and active, and it discerns the thoughts and intents of our hearts (see Heb. 4:12). When everything is laid bare, we are forced to choose how we will respond and whom we will serve.

You search the Scriptures, for in them you think you have eternal life; and these are they which testify of Me. **But you are not willing** *to come to Me that you may have life* (John 5:39-40).

"But you are not willing"—here we see the issue of willingness once again. The Pharisees were willing to go and hear John the Baptist, but they were not willing to encounter Jesus because He challenged their preconceived notions about God. When Jesus showed up on the scene, the hidden realities of their hearts were exposed. The revelation of the God who lays down His life shattered their expectations of greatness and offended their pride. The humility and meekness of this common Man from Nazareth became a stumbling block to those who worshiped grandeur, strength, and success (see Isa. 53:1-3). In the end, the idea of God they formed based on their interpretation of Scripture was an idol that prevented them from recognizing and receiving Jesus.

The heart of the problem lay in the Pharisees' approach to the Word of God: they treated the means as the end. Jesus celebrated their love of the Scriptures, but challenged their assumption that the end goal was knowledge. Though these religious leaders studied the Word of God fervently, they were not willing to open their hearts when confronted with its demands. They searched the Scriptures, but they did not hear the Spirit behind the words and ultimately missed the revelation of Christ. The Word that should have led them to the feet of Jesus instead empowered them to magnify their own ministries and reputation and to lord it over others. These men spent their lives building their own kingdoms, and so when Jesus wouldn't play their religious games and began to shake the foundations of their strongholds, they killed Him.

This is why it is critical to have a right heart posture when we come before the Word of God. Jesus highlights two results that flow from the wrong heart posture. If we do not wage war against them, they will destroy us. They are slavery to the honor and praise of men, and a small heart that does not have the love of God.

> *I do not receive honor from men. But I know you, that you do not have the love of God in you* (John 5:41-42).

The first result is that we get caught in the rat race of competition. When Jesus says He does not receive honor from men, His implication is that we do. Jesus ceases to be our reward and we begin working, striving, and competing for the praise of men. We lose sight of the true end, which is encounter and relationship with God. We no longer evaluate our success based on the tenderness of our heart and our life in the Spirit. The second result is that our hearts become small and are no longer able to receive or give love. Instead of having the love of God in us, we are filled with anger, bitterness, jealousy, self-righteousness, and competition. This is what happens when we opt for simply knowing more than everybody else about the Bible. The way we treat the Word of God, the posture we take before it, and the value we place on it means everything.

THIS IS ETERNAL LIFE

In the next chapter of John, Jesus continues to emphasize the issue of communion and intimacy with God through the Word. This time His target is not the religious elite, but rather the hungry crowd. After Jesus fed the 5,000 with five loaves and two fish, the word got out and His following increased: "The teacher from Nazareth has a soup kitchen—He will hook you up!" But His response is not what we would expect. Instead of being excited that His fame is spreading and the number of disciples is on the rise, Jesus chose to shut down the soup kitchen and challenge the crowd regarding whether they truly understood His words and desired intimacy with Him more than they wanted their needs met.

Who is like Jesus? He waited until He had gathered His biggest crowd, and then He stood up and declared:

Most assuredly, I say to you, unless you eat the flesh of the Son of Man and drink His blood, you have no life in you. Whoever eats My flesh and drinks My blood has eternal life, and I will raise him up at the last day. For My flesh is food indeed, and My blood is drink indeed. He who eats My flesh and drinks My blood abides in Me, and I in him. As the living Father sent Me, and I live because of the Father, so he who feeds on Me will live because of Me (John 6:53-57).

The boldness of this declaration is stunning. Jesus didn't worry about the fact that many in the crowd thought He was endorsing cannibalism. He didn't rush to interpret and explain His teaching. Instead, He let the crowds wrestle with His words. He tested them to see whether they were following Him because they understood His message or because they wanted free food. If they were truly interested in communion, they would press past the offensive words to understand His meaning. This was the indictment: "You don't understand My speech because you are only interested in having your temporal needs met. But this relationship is not about what you want; it's about what I want. I want communion with you. I want to bring you into fellowship, and this will only occur as you eat My flesh and drink My blood."

In response, the disciples complained privately to Jesus: *"This is a hard saying"* (John 6:60). But Jesus was unmoved by popular opinion. He waited for the crowds to reach critical mass before pulling out the most offensive thing He could say, and then repeated it over and over: "Eat My flesh and drink My blood." Jesus desired to meet the temporal needs of the people, but His perspective was eternal and He was more interested in calling them into communion. So He shut down the soup kitchen and created a choice: "Will you continue to be consumed by your needs, or will you persevere in spite of offense and follow Me?"

Jesus set up a scenario that forced the people to choose whether or not they would go deeper in the things of God. Would they leave their comfort behind in order to understand His heart?

Don't get me wrong: I love that God is my Savior, my Provider, my Healer, and my Deliverer. I will never exhaust the glorious gifts that He has given me and continues to give me. I will spend eternity praising Him for my salvation and deliverance, my health and provision. But we have created a church culture in America that is based on feeding the 5,000—we are consumed with the God who meets our needs and do not realize He wants to take us past provision into deeper intimacy. God wants more than a people whose needs are met. He wants a partner; He wants a bride.

At the height of the uproar, Jesus finally began to release insight regarding His true meaning:

> *It is the Spirit who gives life; the flesh profits nothing. The words that I speak to you are spirit, and they are life* (John 6:63).

Eternal life is found in feeding on the words of Jesus. His words contain His very life, and we enter into communion—we eat His flesh and drink His blood—through His words. Even after this clarification, however, there was a great falling away: *"From that time many of His disciples went back and walked with Him no more"* (John 6:66).

> *Then Jesus said to the twelve, "Do you also want to go away?"*

> *But Simon Peter answered Him, "Lord, to whom shall we go? You have the words of eternal life. Also we have come to believe and know that You are the Christ, the Son of the living God"* (John 6:67-69).

As a leader, I would be unnerved by the response of the crowd. If I saw everyone rushing to leave the stadium, I would want to minimize the damage immediately. But Jesus looked at the

12—His closest and most intimate friends—and asked, "Do you want to leave, too?" He gave them a way out, a chance to step back from the cost of discipleship. In Peter's response we see a heart that is postured in hunger and humility before the Word of God. Peter replied, "Jesus, where would we go? We have burned all of our bridges. When we first heard Your words, we left everything to follow You. We live and breathe Your words—they are our life. Your words have caused us to believe that You are the Christ, the Son of the living God."

THE NECESSITY OF THE ABIDING WORD

I want to look at one last passage in John where Jesus confronts the religious leaders over the importance of abiding in the Word. In John 8 He makes one of the greatest statements about the glory of the Word:

If you abide in My word, you are My disciples indeed. And you shall know the truth, and the truth shall make you free (John 8:31-32).

This is not only a significant revelation concerning the power of Scripture, but it is also an invitation extended from the heart of the Father to the religious leaders who continued to reject His Son. In this verse, Jesus revealed the process that leads to freedom. Notice that He said they will *know* the truth. This does not refer to possessing information about the truth; *knowing* is not measured in the ability to repeat facts with accuracy. Instead, knowing refers to experience. Jesus desired to see the Pharisees step into the living experience of freedom—freedom from the slavery of sin—and He declared that this experience begins with abiding in the Word.

A few verses later, Jesus highlighted that they sought to kill Him because His Word had no place in them. Again, He confronted them with the necessity of the abiding Word.

"I know that you are Abraham's descendants, but you seek to kill Me, because My word has no place in you. I speak what I have seen with My Father, and you do what you have seen with your father."

They answered and said to Him, "Abraham is our father."

Jesus said to them, "If you were Abraham's children, you would do the works of Abraham" (John 8:37-39).

Notice that Jesus identified the religious leaders as Abraham's descendants and then went on to say they were not Abraham's children. This is the difference between natural descent and the inheritance of faith. Ishmael and Isaac were both born to Abraham, but only one was born from faith and inherited the promises of God. The Pharisees sought to enter the kingdom based on natural lineage and knowledge. They thought they were children of God because their parents were Jewish and they had studied the Scriptures. But Jesus declared that their inability to receive His words revealed their true heritage. It was not enough to be descendants of Abraham; they needed a heart filled with faith to draw them into true relationship with the Father. Because they did not receive the Word of God, the natural children of Abraham were deceived and demonized. They were sons in the natural, but slaves in the spirit.

Why do you not understand My speech? Because you are not able to listen to My word.... He who is of God hears God's words; therefore you do not hear, because you are not of God (John 8:43,47).

In the final verses of John 8, Jesus revealed that the Pharisees' rejection of God had robbed them of their ability to hear His

Word. They were not able to understand Jesus because they had not learned to listen to the Scriptures. In essence He said, "You do not recognize My speech because the Word is a foreign language to you. You have studied the Scriptures, but you have not learned their language and cultivated a hearing heart. Therefore, My speech does not make sense because you have not engaged in a life of abiding."

This is why Jesus spoke in parables; He came to shut the eyes and close the ears of those who claimed to see and hear clearly. He even stated this explicitly when He quoted the prophet Isaiah concerning His ministry:

> *To you it has been given to know the mystery of the kingdom of God; but to those who are outside, all things come in parables, so that "Seeing they may see and not perceive, and hearing they may hear and not understand"* (Mark 4:11-12).

The sobering truth is that Jesus came to confirm the inward reality of the nation's heart. His words did not cause the people's hardness and inability to hear—they simply revealed it. Though they were God's chosen people, they had not chosen God and were therefore not of God.

THE ROAD TO ENCOUNTER

The vital thing is the living encounter with the God who speaks to us in his Word, whose eyes pierce and purify us "like a flame of fire" (Rev 1:14), whose command summons us to new obedience, who each day instructs us as if until now we had learned nothing, whose power sends us out anew into the world upon our mission. Unless he responds by such obedience to the free word of God in him, man is not living up to the idea which God the Father had of him at creation.[4]

In the economy of the kingdom, the most important and valuable thing is living encounter with the Word. Jesus charged the Pharisees again and again concerning their heart posture before the Word of God because He desired to see them experience freedom and enter into communion. Through His interactions with these men, we are given a mirror by which to examine our own lives. How do we relate to the Word? What is our heart posture when we approach Scripture—how do we read it, treat it, look at it? Do we stand over the Word, or do we allow the Word to stand over us? The Word of God is meant to escort us into the realities of the Spirit. It is meant to bring us into a new paradigm, a new way of experiencing and relating to the emotions, thoughts, and plans of God, producing in us a heart inflamed with divine love. The end is a divine confrontation with Jesus that strips us of our religious rhetoric and hypocrisy, and leaves us bowing in humility with a heart awakened to revelation.

As we stated in the first chapter, Jeremiah declared that the people of Judah were not able to hear because they did not delight in the Word of God (see Jer. 6:10). Delighting in the Word is the secret to the restoration of hearing. When we come through the door of delight, our defenses are broken down and we become vulnerable to truth, which eventually leads to full submission and humility before the Word. In the next chapter we are going to look at the place where God broke down all of my walls and captivated my heart—the place of joy and delight in His Word.

Chapter 4

DELIGHTING IN THE WORD

When I was in my early 20s, I had a job at a factory working the second shift. The days were long and the work was draining, but I look back on that time in my life as one of the most significant seasons in God I have ever experienced. I would go to the factory, sit on the assembly line, and meditate on the Word of God. Throughout the day, verses and individual phrases from Scripture would rest on my spirit and my heart would begin to burn: *"Oh, how I love Your law! It is my meditation all the day"* (Ps. 119:97). In the midst of the daily grind, I discovered that I was made to live and breathe and feel the Word. I may have been physically present in the factory, but my heart was lost in meditation for hours on end. In that season of working, I found the true source of life. I found the Word that started a fire within me, which still burns to this day.

DAVID: A MAN AFTER GOD'S OWN HEART

I want to spend some time looking at my favorite chapter in the Bible: Psalm 119.[1] In this psalm, David pulls back the curtains of his heart and we are given a glimpse into the deep love affair he had with the Word of God. Though he was one of the wealthiest and most powerful men of his day, ambition was not the central motivation of his life. Instead, it was a deep and abiding love for God and a desire for His Word—a desire that characterized his life from beginning to end. Acts 13:22 identifies David as a man after God's own heart, a man who fulfilled the will of God in his generation.

There are many additional titles and accomplishments that can be added to David's résumé. With the exception of the life of Christ, his story is the longest personal narrative recorded in the Scriptures. He was the divinely anointed king of Israel who was promised an eternal royal lineage (see 2 Sam. 7:12-16). He was a military hero who conquered giants and surrounding nations. He expanded his territory until the people of Israel occupied nearly all the land promised to their forefather Abraham. He returned the Ark of the Covenant to its rightful place in Jerusalem and restored the spirit of worship across the land. For all these reasons and more, he is considered to be one of the greatest leaders Israel has ever known. As one scholar observes, "A thousand years after his death, when Jesus rode into Jerusalem, the most glorious name the people could think to call him was 'Son of David!' (Matt. 21:9)."[2]

However, I believe it was his consuming passion to experience the heart of God that truly defined him. David was a man after one thing. What brought joy to others failed to bring him joy. What the world defined as success did not impress him. He found his joy, success, and identity in a different place—he found it in encountering God through His Word. In Psalm 27 David declared:

> One thing I have desired of the Lord, that will I seek: that I may dwell in the house of the Lord all the days of my life, to

behold the beauty of the Lord, and to inquire in His temple (Psalm 27:4).

I can almost hear David asking us in this psalm, "Do you want to know what ultimately motivates and drives me when nobody else is watching? Do you want to know the overwhelming desire that fills my heart night and day? The greatest desire in my life is to be closer to God and to see Him more than any other. Take my kingdom. Take my fortune. Take my military might—you can take everything as long as I have this one thing. My greatest fear in life is not losing my reputation or my power; it is losing His face."

David's request to dwell in the house of the Lord expressed his desire to draw closer to God. His desire to behold the beauty of the Lord, which is His nature and personality, expressed his longing for the knowledge of God. He knew his heart would fail without fresh revelation, a greater sense of God's abiding presence, and deeper communion. This is what David cried out to behold, and this cry sustained him throughout his life. For David, the pay was the same whether he was on the backside of a hill in Bethlehem or on the throne in Jerusalem. It didn't matter to him, as long as he could encounter God. It was this foundation in the Word that strengthened and encouraged him when he was overlooked and rejected by his family while tending the flocks in Bethlehem. It was intimacy with the Word that helped him persevere through the numerous trials he faced as the leader of his people. The secret to David's life was found in enjoying the Word of God and loving it more than anything else in life.

PSALM 119

While David proclaims the greatest desire of his heart in Psalm 27, it is Psalm 119 that reveals the depths of that desire. In the Song of Solomon, the maiden declares concerning her beloved, *"Let him kiss me with the kisses of his mouth"* (Song of Sol. 1:2a). We see in Proverbs 2:6 that knowledge and understanding come from the mouth of God, and so when we view the Song of Solomon through the lens of Christ and the church, we understand that this is a cry for the revelation of the Word of God.

I believe that Psalm 119 is the ultimate commentary on the cry for the kisses of the Word. In this psalm, David displays the heart and mind of a lover who carefully searches out their beloved as he uses 176 verses to declare his passion for the Word. It is his delight, his pleasure, his place of enjoyment, his source of satisfaction, his defense, his only comfort, and the wellspring of his life. We hear David's desire for revelation and the kisses of God's Word in every verse.

Many of us, if we are honest, think of Psalm 119 as the boring chapter we try to avoid. The most common complaints are that it is too long and that it says the same thing over and over again. Charles Spurgeon, in his commentary on this psalm, addresses these very complaints:

> This great Psalm is a book in itself: instead of being one among many psalms, it is worthy to be set forth by itself as a poem of surpassing excellence. Those who have never studied it may pronounce it commonplace, and complain of its repetitions; but to the thoughtful student it is like the great deep, full, so as never to be measured; and varied, so as never to weary the eye. Its depth is as great as its length; it is mystery, not set forth as mystery, but concealed beneath the simplest statements...[3]

> Using only a few words, the writer has produced permutations and combination of meaning which display his holy familiarity with his subject, and the sanctified ingenuity of his mind. He never repeats himself; for if

the same sentiment recurs it is placed in a fresh connection, and so exhibits another interesting shade of meaning…. It contains no idle word; the grapes of this cluster are almost to bursting full with the new wine of the kingdom. The more you look into this mirror of a gracious heart the more you will see in it. Placid on the surface as the sea of glass before the eternal throne, it yet contains within its depths an ocean of fire, and those who devoutly gaze into it shall not only see the brightness, but feel the glow of the sacred flame.[4]

Matthew Henry, a theologian and minister of the 17th century best known for publishing a commentary on the entire Bible, recounts how his father recommended he read Psalm 119 in order to cultivate a love for the Scriptures:

Once pressing the Study of the Scriptures, he advised to take a Verse of Psalm 119 every Morning to meditate upon, and so go over the Psalm twice in the year, and that (saith he) will bring you to be in love with all the rest of the Scripture; and he often said, All grace grows, as love to the Word of God grows [sic].[5]

Psalm 119 is, in essence, a lengthy acrostic poem written in praise of the Scriptures. It is composed of 22 stanzas—one for each letter of the Hebrew alphabet. The stanzas themselves are composed of eight couplets. As you read through the psalm, you will notice that David uses ten different terms for the Word of God: law, way, testimony, precept, statute, commandments, judgment, word, saying, and truth. While each term carries a different shade of meaning, I find it helpful to remind myself that they all constitute the communications of God's heart to mine through His Word.

We often forget that David was reading through the Torah when he wrote this psalm. He was reading about the priesthood, with all of its laws and regulations, and falling madly in love with God. In response to Leviticus, he said, *"And I will delight myself in Your commandments, which I love"* (Ps. 119:47). He was captivated by the revelation of God's heart as he read through the book of Numbers. What did he discover as he meditated on the Book of the Law?

THE MAIN INTERPRETATIVE KEY OF PSALM 119

Blessed are the undefiled in the way, who walk in the law of the Lord! Blessed are those who keep His testimonies, who seek Him with the whole heart! (Psalm 119:1-2)

The first word of Psalm 119 is *blessed*. This word actually means "happy" or "to be envied," and it characterizes the entire psalm. David began by declaring that the happiest people are those who give their whole hearts to the Word of God. Notice that he doesn't rebuke or dismiss the longing for happiness, but instead gives us the secret to attaining it. Everyone wants to be happy; it is a God-given desire. In our hearts we know we were made for enjoyment—it is what our culture is crying out for and what we spend our entire lives pursuing. Our generation longs for pleasure, fascination, and entertainment, and many will stop at nothing to attain it.

The desire for happiness is behind many multibillion-dollar industries: the film industry, the sports industry, the fashion industry, and the food industry, to name just a few. According to one research and consulting company, the film industry in North America is expected to generate $40.8 billion in revenue in 2012, and they project that this will grow to $50.3 billion by 2015.[6] This is just one example of how desperate we are for fascination and comfort. Our consumer culture and the insatiable material- ism it encourages is another telling example: in 2011, total U.S.

consumer debt equaled $2.43 trillion and the average credit card debt per household was $15,799.[7] These numbers represent the search for happiness through the accumulation of possessions.

Not only are entertainment and materialism stealing our time, energy, and resources, but the spirit of immorality is working to quench our hearts and prevent us from encountering the Word of God. The onslaught of sexual immorality and pornography in our nation is an assignment from hell to dull our spirits and cut off the power of the Word. Estimates vary, but the general consensus is that the pornography industry generates between $10 and $14 billion in revenue each year. This epidemic is destroying our ability to recognize and experience true pleasure. Thomas Dubay writes with great insight about the experience of men and women who spend their money and their lives in pursuit of happiness:

> Unrest is the omnipresent accompaniment of earthly pursuits, and anyone who has lived a few years into adulthood and is therefore capable of a rudimentary reflection on the human situation knows well from experience that nothing fully satisfies. Soon after even peak experiences one begins to feel the inner gnawing emptiness…. Because spirit as spirit opens to the infinite, it can be satisfied and rested only in the infinite. All else leaves it incomplete and desiring more.[8]

In other words, it is never enough. Our desire for happiness cannot be met by anything this world has to offer. As Augustine wrote in his *Confessions*, "Thou madest us for Thyself, and our heart is restless, until it rest in Thee."[9] This is why David begins Psalm 119 by declaring that holiness is the only true and infinite source of happiness. We won't find what we are looking for in the accumulation of possessions or in overindulgence. David identifies the happiest people as those who are "undefiled in the way" and "whole-hearted seekers of God's Word." Happiness and holiness characterize our lives when God becomes more pleasurable than anything this world has to offer. Holiness is not primarily about saying no to the things of the world; it is about saying yes to the superior pleasures of loving God. David is not describing a heart that begrudgingly says no to sin and the world. The happiest ones are the holiest ones. This is the paradigm we need in order to approach Psalm 119.

The greatest discovery that impacted me in this psalm, as a new believer, was that there was a source of entertainment, fascination, pleasure, comfort, joy, and counsel that nothing in this world could equal. I began to realize that my primary source of entertainment was the Word of God, and my greatest joy was not found in indulging in the pleasures of this age. Through meditating on Psalm 119, I discovered happy holiness. As I read, I began to experience deep and abiding joy, the wine of the Spirit, the unshakeable peace that comes from a clean conscience, and the burning heart described in the encounter with Jesus on the road to Emmaus. I came from a drug and party lifestyle, yet I found that nothing from my previous life touched or equaled my experiences in the Word of God. My greatest pleasure was the Word. I didn't want to do those other things anymore—it wasn't about saying no, it was about saying yes.

I believe that just as He delivered me, God is delivering our generation from the entertainment of this world through the superior pleasures of His Word. Day after day, month after month, and year after year, we are being transformed by our encounters with heaven. These encounters are stronger than anything this world has to offer. Nothing is as satisfying, intoxicating, fulfilling, and vital as God communicating His Word to our spirits.

> He alone is the Bread of Life for which our souls hunger; we need not go any further, looking for any other bread, for its spiritual satisfaction would be illusory. He suffices.[10]

I don't know when or how it happened, but God brought Psalm 119 to the forefront of my life. I remember spending entire days in my room after I was first saved, slowly reading and meditating upon this chapter and falling in love with the God who speaks to me in His Word. Over 15 years have passed since then, but I still return to this psalm when I feel God calling me back to my first love (see Rev. 2:4-5).

Over the course of many years, I have found several main themes which have helped me to interpret and connect with the heart behind this psalm. I want to share these with you and provide a brief commentary on specific verses God has used to powerfully touch my life. My hope is that you will take the ideas behind this commentary and use them to begin your own dialogue with the Lord. As you read the verses below, stop and softly speak them back to the Lord. Add a few sentences of your own that express the truth of the psalmist's lines, and ask the Holy Spirit to open your heart to receive the kisses of His Word.

HAPPY HOLINESS

Again, Charles Spurgeon says,

> The Psalmist is so enraptured with the word of God that he regards it as his highest ideal of blessedness to be conformed to it. He has gazed on the beauties of the perfect law, and, as if this verse were the sum and outcome of all his emotions, he exclaims, "Blessed is the man whose life is the practical transcript of the will of God." True religion is not cold and dry; it has its exclamations and raptures. We not only judge the keeping of God's law to be a wise and proper thing, but we are warmly enamoured of its holiness, and cry out in adoring wonder, "Blessed are the undefiled!" meaning thereby, that we eagerly desire to become

such ourselves, and wish for no greater happiness than to be perfectly holy.[11]

Open my eyes, that I may see wondrous things from Your law (Psalm 119:18).

Like the cry of the poor, blind beggar who arrested Jesus' attention, may this cry release sight to my heart in the Word. I pray with Paul, "That the God of our Lord Jesus Christ, the Father of glory, may give to me the spirit of wisdom and revelation in the knowledge of Him, *the eyes of my understanding being enlightened*" (Eph. 1:17-18 paraphrased). I pray that wonder would be restored to my heart as my eyes are opened to the Word.

The law of Your mouth is better to me than thousands of coins of gold and silver (Psalm 119:72).

Your love is better than anything this world has to offer. Receiving Your love is more valuable to me than the treasures of this life.

How sweet are Your words to my taste, sweeter than honey to my mouth! (Psalm 119:103)

I have developed a spiritual taste for Your Word, and it is sweeter, more satisfying, and more gratifying than the pleasures this world has to offer.

Your testimonies are wonderful; therefore my soul keeps them (Psalm 119:129).

Because I have experienced true wonder, my soul jealously guards Your Word.

I rejoice at Your word as one who finds great treasure (Psalm 119:162).

In the same way that a treasure hunter finds the purpose of his life in searching for riches, so my soul finds life and redemption in discovering Your Word. Your Word brings me the greatest joy, therefore I will hold on to it eternally.

...And Your law is my delight (Psalm 119:174).

I want the Word to become my chief source of entertainment and delight. I want meditation in the Word to be my getaway, my escape, my source of recreation and rest.

LONGING FOR BREAKTHROUGH

> God is not truly sought by the cold researches of the brain: we must seek him with the heart. Love reveals itself to love: God manifests his heart to the heart of his people. It is in vain that we endeavour to comprehend him by reason; we must apprehend him by affection. But the heart must not be divided with many objects if the Lord is to be sought by us. God is one, and we shall not know him till our heart is one. A broken heart need not be distressed at this, for no heart is so whole in its seekings after God as a heart which is broken, whereof every fragment sighs and cries after the great Father's face. It is the divided heart which the doctrine of the text censures, and strange to say, in scriptural phraseology, a heart may be divided and not broken, and it may be broken but not divided; and yet again it may be broken and be whole, and it never can be whole until it is broken.[12]

How can a young man cleanse his way? (Psalm 119:9)

A young man is at the height of his passion, rebellion, and curiosity. Similarly, our generation is experiencing heightened internal temptation as we are exposed to every imaginable external temptation in a culture saturated with entertainment, perversion, voices, and images—all pulling us away from the straight and narrow road. We desperately need to know how to cleanse our past, present, and future. How can we live in purity? The psalmist answers, *"By taking heed according to Your word"* (Ps. 119:9). May I be wholly attentive to and governed by the Word of God.

> *My soul breaks with longing for Your judgments at all times* (Psalm 119:20).

I am desperate to see all the wrong things made right in my soul. Your Word has awakened a longing in my life for deeper measures of truth (see Ps. 51:6). Come and align my heart, my mind, and my will according to Your judgments.

> *Turn away my eyes from looking at worthless things, and revive me in Your way* (Psalm 119:37).

I feel the pull of other lovers, but my heart's cry is for a life of revival in Your Word. I do not want to turn my eyes alone. Come and turn the very core of my being fully toward You.

> *I opened my mouth and panted, for I longed for Your commandments* (Psalm 119:131).

Just as the deer pants for the water brooks (see Ps. 42:1), so I pant for fresh encounter in the Word. God, I am thirsty for You.

> *I cry out with my whole heart; hear me, O Lord!* (Psalm 119:145)

Desperate times call for desperate measures: I am seeking You with all my heart and will not relent until You answer me.

> *I rise before the dawning of the morning, and cry for help; I hope in Your word. My eyes are awake through the night watches, that I may meditate on Your word* (Psalm 119:147-148).

May my heart be awake both night and day, meditating upon and hoping in Your Word.

WHOLEHEARTED DEPENDENCE

God must work in us first, and then we shall will and do according to his good pleasure. He must change the heart, unite the heart, encourage the heart, strengthen the heart, and enlarge the heart, and then the course of the life will be gracious, sincere, happy, and earnest; so that from our lowest up to our highest state in grace we must attribute all to the free favour of our God. We must run; for grace is not an overwhelming force which compels unwilling minds to move contrary to their will: our running is the spontaneous leaping forward of a mind which has been set free by the hand of God, and delights to show its freedom by its bounding speed.[13]

At the core of Psalm 119 is a necessary tension. On the one hand, we are called again and again to seek God wholeheartedly and to give Him all of our heart, soul, mind, and strength. However, we are also reminded of our inability to do anything without God.

With my whole heart I have sought You; oh, let me not wander from Your commandments! (Psalm 119:10)

I am wholeheartedly and desperately seeking You, but I know my propensity to stray from Your Word!

I am a stranger in the earth; do not hide Your commandments from me (Psalm 119:19).

I am not of this world, and this world is not my home. Do not keep my very life source from me.

I will run the course of Your commandments, for You shall enlarge my heart (Psalm 119:32).

I will not wait for my life circumstances to line up before I pursue You wholeheartedly. I will seek Your kingdom first, and trust that You will enlarge my heart and make a way for me in the midst of my circumstances. I will go where You tell me to go as I receive fresh encounters.

> *Uphold me according to Your word, that I may live; and do not let me be ashamed of my hope. Hold me up, and I shall be safe, and I shall observe Your statutes continually* (Psalm 119:116-117).

It is Your mercy that allows me to live in obedience, free from shame and filled with hope.

> *I have gone astray like a lost sheep; seek Your servant, for I do not forget Your commandments* (Psalm 119:176).

I know my propensity is to stray. Come after me, and keep me from wandering and growing weary or distracted.

THE FREEDOM OF A PREOCCUPIED HEART

In Psalm 119, David reveals the secret of possessing a free heart in the midst of persecution. There are numerous instances recorded in First and Second Samuel where David was spiritually, verbally, and physically attacked by those around him. However, he refused to let these attacks become his primary meditation. His thoughts were consumed with the Word of God: *"Princes also sit and speak against me, but Your servant meditates on Your statutes"* (Ps. 119:23). What is your greatest preoccupation? Is it what others think of you, or is it what God says in His Word?

> *...they treated me wrongfully with falsehood; but I will meditate on Your precepts* (Psalm 119:78).

I have been wronged, but I will let You be my defense. While they talk about me behind my back, I'll be preoccupied with meditating on Your Word.

The wicked wait for me to destroy me, but I will consider Your testimonies (Psalm 119:95).

They are waiting to catch me, trip me up, and destroy me, but I am not moving my gaze away from Your Word.

Many are my persecutors and my enemies, yet I do not turn from Your testimonies (Psalm 119:157).

The enemy has many assignments against me, but I will not be moved.

Princes persecute me without a cause, but my heart stands in awe of Your word (Psalm 119:161).

In the midst of persecution, I am preoccupied with the glory of Your Word.

Great peace have those who love Your law, and nothing causes them to stumble (Psalm 119:165).

My heart is not in the hands of men's opinions; it is hidden in You.

THE FRUIT OF AFFLICTION

Very little is to be learned without affliction. If we would be scholars we must be sufferers…. God's commands are best read by eyes wet with tears.[14]

Another main theme found in this psalm is the power of affliction to drive us deeper into the Word of God. Many times God uses pain and to produce sensitivity to the Word in our hearts.

Before I was afflicted I went astray, but now I keep Your word (Psalm 119:67).

I used to leave Your commandments so quickly, but now I have been hemmed in through affliction and have learned that my true safety is found in being near You.

It is good for me that I have been afflicted, that I may learn Your statutes (Psalm 119:71).

I know, O Lord, that Your judgments are right, and that in faithfulness You have afflicted me (Psalm 119:75).

All Your judgments are true and righteous. I trust You and know that You are leading me down this difficult road for my good.

Unless Your law had been my delight, I would then have perished in my affliction (Psalm 119:92).

If Your Word was not the main joy of my life, I would not have made it through this last season.

Consider my affliction and deliver me, for I do not forget Your law (Psalm 119:153).

Lord, look at me and deliver me, for I am clinging to You.

THE REVIVING POWER OF THE WORD

Troubles which weigh us down while we are half dead become mere trifles when we are full of life. Thus have we often been raised in spirit by quickening grace, and the same thing will happen again, for the Comforter is still with us, the Consolation of Israel ever liveth, and the very God of peace is evermore our Father. On looking back upon our past life there is one ground of comfort as to our state—the word of God has made us alive, and kept us so. We were dead, but we are dead no longer.[15]

The last main theme of Psalm 119 is the power of the Word of God to release life in our inner being and revive our soul. This theme is repeated in verse 52 when David states, *"I remembered Your judgments of old, O Lord, and have comforted myself."* In other words, "I have seen what You did in the past, and it has comforted my soul with the revelation that You are the God of the breakthrough. I know what You did for Moses, and that knowledge comforts me." We have to remember as we read through this psalm that David pulled from all of his life experiences when composing it. He knew what it was like to hide in the cave of Adullam (see 1 Sam. 22), he was familiar with being pushed and pulled by the needs and demands of others, and as the king of Israel he was constantly under enormous pressure. But in every season of the soul, the Word of God had the power to renew and refresh him.

…Revive me in Your way (Psalm 119:37).

…Revive me in Your righteousness (Psalm 119:40).

Revive me according to Your lovingkindness… (Psalm 119:88).

…Revive me, O Lord, according to Your word (Psalm 119:107).

…Revive me according to Your word (Psalm 119:154).

…Revive me according to Your judgments (Psalm 119:156).

…Revive me, O Lord, according to Your lovingkindness (Psalm 119:159).

Whenever I feel disconnected from God, I return to Psalm 119. The Word of God was the place where David went for fresh encounter, and it is where I go to reawaken my first love.

When was the last time prayer began to spontaneously arise from within you as you read the Bible? When was the last time you actually talked to God as you meditated on His Word? The answer to these questions is the litmus test I use to determine where I am with God. Is my heart moving when I read the Word? Am I weeping as I read it? When did I last feel the wine of His presence refresh and rejoice my heart? When was the last time I received a fresh touch of the spirit of revelation and began to feel fascination that wasn't related to the things of this world? If our heart response to the Word of God is weariness and familiarity, if we find ourselves wondering when we can move on to something else, it is the very indictment of our need for the Word.

In the next several chapters I want to share with you some of the ways God has brought me into a life of meditation in the Word. We will look at biblical truths designed to help us posture our hearts to receive from the Word, and we will also explore practical tools to equip us in our times of meditation. Slowing down and meditating on the Word of God has changed my life. It has not only been my greatest source of joy, but it has also been the source of my obedience, faith, and sacrifice.

As I stated in the first chapter, there is a great need for the body of Christ to rediscover the ancient paths—the place of silence where we encounter the Word and it becomes our delight. Many of us perpetually live in a dry, difficult season when it comes to the Bible. However, in Jeremiah 31 the prophet declares that we were made to feel the Word of God:

> But this is the covenant that I will make with the house of Israel after those days, says the Lord: I will put My law in their minds, and write it on their hearts; and I will be their God, and they shall be My people (Jeremiah 31:33).

This is our inheritance; the Word of God is meant to touch our thought life and our emotions. All we need to do is slow down and shift our approach.

Chapter 5

BREAKING THROUGH THE PAGES

The most significant breakthrough in the revelation of the love of God I have ever experienced came through meditating on the Word of God. The verse that changed my life was John 17:24, where Jesus prays:

> *Father, I desire that they also whom You gave Me may be with Me where I am, that they may behold My glory which You have given Me; for You loved Me before the foundation of the world.*

For six months I couldn't read anything else. Every time I opened the Bible, I would find myself held captive by *"Father, I desire..."* This verse occurs near the end of what is known as the High Priestly Prayer of Jesus. In the midst of His final teaching before the cross, Jesus shared with the Father the deepest longings of His heart as He prayed for His disciples and for all those who would believe in Him throughout the coming generations. When we read this prayer, we are hearing God the Son talk to God the Father by the power of God the Spirit, and we are allowed to listen to this holy conversation that unveils the heart of the Trinity. Somewhere between the Passover table and the Garden of Gethsemane, the God who needs nothing revealed His overwhelming desire for me.

Every day I would wake up, grab my coffee, and think to myself, "Corey, flight John 17:24 is taking off into the heart of God this morning. Do you want to get on?" I would picture myself boarding a plane as I began to read; this verse was a vehicle of encounter, piloted by the Holy Spirit, which took me into the atmosphere of the emotions, thoughts, and plans of God. The more time I spent reading it, the more I discovered that the words *"Father, I desire"* contained an endless revelation of God. John 17:24 unlocked the bridal paradigm for me. I began to see that the God who created the heavens and the earth wanted something: He desired from before the foundation of the world that I would be with Him where He is, beholding His glory. Suddenly I began to understand the motivation that sent Jesus to the cross. I was raised in the church and knew what happened at Calvary. But what I didn't know was the passionate heart of God that sent Jesus to Calvary for me.

Before that season of meditation on John 17:24, my relationship with God was like watching a 20-inch black and white television that only receives three channels. But when I started to ask questions about the context of the verse and about the significance and power of the prayer Jesus offered the night before He was crucified, I began to enter into the story. I became a participant in the drama of John 17:24. I watched Jesus praying and heard Him ask the Father for *me*. I used to see God as a stoic, detached Being; but when I heard Jesus declaring that He wanted me to be with Him, that 20-inch television became a 60-inch high definition plasma screen with hundreds of channels. God came alive to me. The Bible opened up and I saw that from Genesis to Revelation, God was pursuing me. When I connected with this revelation, I realized the entire Bible could be summed up by the word *desire*.

I began to wrestle over the meaning of *desire* and realized that it is neither casual nor passive. It doesn't sound like, "Boy, it would be nice if I had this." Desire is a craving, a longing, a demand of the soul for gratification. Desire declares, "I absolutely must have this or I will die." As I meditated on the nature of desire, that word became a world of revelation, understanding, and emotion within me. Desire began to absorb and consume me. God rearranged my mind and emotions, and I fell in love. I was no longer trying to get God's attention; I was swimming in an ocean called desire. My soul was baptized into the experiential reality of God's heart. In the past I would have identified myself as a worker in the kingdom. Now I knew that I was a lover and a friend. I could state with confidence for the first time that I was not created to live from a sense of duty; I was created to live in response to God's overwhelming love, longing to surrender everything to Him.

When I look back on the six months I spent meditating on John 17:24, I picture this verse as a ship resting on the surface of the ocean. At first I only saw the cabins, compartments, timber, and sails that comprised the ship, but there was an ocean of revelation under the vessel. As I was patient and lingered over each word, I eventually broke through into the depths of John 17:24. It took more than a few days; it took weeks and months of patiently reading and rereading those same words before the Holy Spirit escorted me beyond mental understanding and into the Word itself, into the shoreless ocean called the knowledge of God. By the end of those six months, desire was more than a Bible verse to me; it was a reality. I was drowning in impartation, revelation, and transformation.

I remember my introduction to meditation and contemplation. A friend of mine gave me the book *Fire Within* by Thomas Dubay—an account of some of the most famous contemplatives in church history. As soon as I started reading this book, I began to experience the manifestation of the fire of God. During the next two months, this spirit of burning rested on me both physically and spiritually, often for six to eight hours each day, and the Word of God was exploding within me. At times I did not think I could handle it. The experience was totally foreign and overwhelming, and I did not understand what was happening. Looking back, I now understand that God was releasing a supernatural season of encounter to escort me into His Word. I have never forgotten the realm of fire available to us if we will say yes to meditation and allow the Spirit to touch our hearts through the Word.

This experience is available through every verse. The Bible is an entire world, and if we move beyond simply reading, the revelation within the Word will overtake and transform our lives. There is so much more than information available to us contained within its pages. We can engage with Christ, fill ourselves with His Spirit, eat His flesh and drink His blood, and truly enter into communion. When we receive breakthrough at that level, it feels as though no other verse exists. Revelation is like putting on a pair of glasses; our hearts and minds see everything through this new lens. When I had a revelation of desire in John 17:24, suddenly I saw desire *everywhere*. Those three words changed my life.

A FOUNDATIONAL PARADIGM SHIFT

My immersion in John 17:24 did more than transform my heart—it shifted my paradigm when it came to reading and studying the Bible. I used to only read for information, but now I also came looking for impartation and encounter. I had unwittingly stumbled upon the secret of meditation, and to my surprise it wasn't a technique I applied while reading or a discipline I practiced during my quiet times (although techniques and disciplines can be valuable tools, and we will look at both in the following chapters). The secret was a shift in the motivation of my heart, and a willingness to slow down.

I am a product of my culture—a fast-paced guy who likes to get things done. But for six months I could only read these three words over and over: *"Father, I desire…"* Have you ever been driving down the road when a maniac suddenly races by at 90 mph? All you can do is yell, "Slow down!" Often, that is what the Holy Spirit is saying to us when we read the Bible. He is saying, "Slow down. I want to impart the knowledge of God to you. I want to reveal Myself through these words. I want to encounter and transform you."

The curse of Western culture is the fast pace at which we live. Many of us say, "I know John 17:24 because I have read through the Gospels and completed my memory verses." Memory verses are a great way to get the Word in your mouth and in your head, but it can't stop there. The Word has to move into your heart and your prayer life. Don't say, "I know that verse." Ask yourself if the verse knows you. Does John 17:24 know you? Would that verse say, "Yeah, I have been hanging out with him," or would it say, "No, I don't really know him. I've seen him run right by me a few times."

I believe the Lord is calling each of us to slow down. He wants to deliver us from our performance-driven culture that boasts in the ability to read the Bible in a year, and that places its confidence in completing scheduled quiet times. The God of desire doesn't just want us to check Him off a list; He wants to fill us with the knowledge of His will. The Word contains the very DNA of God. Each phrase is a divine door into the realm of the Spirit. What would happen if we didn't read our Bibles in a year? What would happen if we began to fill our spirits with individual words and phrases from the Scriptures, and it penetrated deeper than our minds? The Word of God is meant to go down into the depths of our souls so that we actually feel it burning within us and becoming our reality.

I stated this in an earlier chapter, but it bears repeating: the Word of God is a means, not an end. It is a means unto encountering the Word made flesh and possessing a heart inflamed with love for God. The end is a divine confrontation with the Word who looks past our rhetoric, hypocrisy, and religious forms—the Word who sees us as we really are and still desires us. But we will not receive this encounter if we do not move beyond performance and stop filling our minds while neglecting our hearts.

We live in a society that teaches us to live for the test. One of the primary things I learned in school was how to do only what was required of me. I was an expert at cramming the night before the test. I would stay up all night studying for a chemistry test, walk into class the next morning, and spit everything in my short-term memory bank on to the paper. I would ace the test, but if you asked me a question about chemistry two days later, I wouldn't have a clue what you were talking about. I learned the information for the sake of a grade. I deceived myself into thinking that I knew something about chemistry, but in reality nothing had changed and I left everything I thought I knew behind me in that classroom.

Many of us relate to the Word of God this way. We read it because we know we are supposed to and we want to avoid the hot seat. We cram the night before the test and spit the information back out, but it never impacts us or moves inside of us to the point where we become victims apprehended by something real, powerful, and alive. The Word is a Person who is after us; He wants to own us, possess us, and transform us. This is unlike science and chemistry and math and English. We have to change our paradigm and the way we do our assignments. We cannot read the Bible just to do it. If that is our approach, the information will never reach our hearts. We will own it instead of allowing it to own us. We must slow down to actually let the Word enlighten and awaken us. We must take our time if we want to fill our souls as well as our minds.

THE NECESSARY HEART POSTURE

So how should we approach the Word of God? What does it look like to sit down and actually engage in meditation? Now that we have established the necessity and the rewards of encountering God in His Word, it is time to look at the practical steps that will lead us into encounter. I have stated this multiple times, but it needs to be said again: the first step is to slow down and quiet your heart. Mike Bickle, the founder and director of the International House of Prayer, uses the metaphor of a menu to describe the importance of slowing down when we read the Word of God.

> You can starve to death reading the menu. Passages of Scripture read quickly or at an introductory, surface level present us with the menu—the rich food available to those who will drink deeply and meditate. Many believers only talk about the menu; some read it and become connoisseurs of the menu. But few actually eat from the menu.[1]

Determine in your heart that you will not merely fulfill your daily Bible reading plan, but will seek to encounter the Person behind the verses. You may feel unproductive at first, but don't let this convince you to move on. As you slow down, verses will begin to jump off the page and grab your attention. When this happens, take a breath and focus on those verses. Then stay there. That is the first step.

The second step is to correctly posture your heart as you read. The Lord shows us in Proverbs 2 how we must come before Him in order to receive all that He has for us.

My son, if you receive my words, and treasure my commands within you, so that you incline your ear to wisdom, and apply your heart to understanding; yes, if you cry out for discernment, and lift up your voice for understanding, if you seek her as silver, and search for her as for hidden treasures; then you will understand the fear of the Lord, and find the knowledge of God (Proverbs 2:1-5).

Here we see three conditions that, if fulfilled, will help us move the knowledge of God from our heads into our hearts. We can receive volumes of information about God, but unless we enter into the realities of Proverbs 2, that information will never become life-giving revelation. The first condition is receiving and treasuring the Word of God. The second is crying out for revelation; while the third is seeking and searching for the Word as for hidden treasure. If we walk in these, we are promised breakthrough in the knowledge of God. Many believers pursue only one of these realities, but all three are needed—we are in need of a contemplative heart that quietly receives the Word of God, and a holy violence that cries out for breakthrough in intercession.

Receiving and treasuring the Word of God describes the heart posture of one who quiets his or her soul and sits before the Word in meditation and contemplation. Luke 10:38-42 illustrates this powerfully. You know the story: when Jesus visited Martha and Mary, Martha ran around serving and working while Mary sat at His feet and heard His word. Her humble desire to listen and receive moved Jesus to declare that she had chosen the one thing necessary in life, and that she would hold on to what she received eternally. Mary discovered the truth that all believers are primarily called to be recipients of the Word of God. We do not have to physically kneel as she did, but we are called to carry our hearts with the understanding that God has invited us into a holy place of encounter where we sit at His feet and receive His Word.

Hans Urs von Balthasar comments on these verses:

> The attention which Mary gave to Jesus, sitting at his feet, was by no means a personal indulgence or a pleasant daydreaming. Nor was it a selective groping for those ideas which suited her, which she "felt able" to translate into reality, let alone pass on to others as her ideas. It was an entirely open-ended readiness for the Word, a readiness to participate in it, without preferences, without picking and choosing, without a priori restrictions. It was an alert, sober attitude, attentive to the slightest indications, yet ready to embrace the widest panoramas.[2]

If *receiving* speaks of the heart posture of Mary of Bethany— a heart that sits underneath the Word in quietness, humility, and openness—then *treasuring* speaks of the value placed on the Word by the hearer. Many of us need a new value system when it comes to the Word of God. Often we are too casual with the revelation we receive; we don't stop to thank the Lord for opening our ears, and we quickly forget what He said. We must learn to hold the Word in our hearts as a priceless possession and return to the Lord with overflowing gratitude, asking for more understanding.

The second condition is crying out for discernment and understanding. This describes the heart posture of one who is desperate for breakthrough. This crying out is a manifestation of the gift of hunger. *The Gospels make one thing very clear: hungry people get things from Jesus that others do not.* The Canaanite woman, blind Bartimaeus, the woman with the issue of blood—each of them pressed through overwhelming internal and external obstacles in their desperation for God, and each received gifts from Jesus that otherwise would never have been released. This is why the greatest gift that can be given to the human spirit is the gift of hunger: *"Blessed are those who hunger and thirst for righteousness, for they shall be filled"* (Matt. 5:6). It doesn't say the blessing is for those who are filled. No, the blessing is for the weak and empty, those who are desperate and on the verge of breaking.

Notice that we are called to sit at the feet of Jesus, hearing His Word, but we are also called to violent intercession fueled by hunger. In the Song of Solomon, the maiden searches for her beloved in the familiar places of comfort and ease represented by her room. But when she cannot find him, she rises from her bed and relentlessly searches the city (see Song of Sol. 3:1-4). We can summarize her journey thus: "I am looking for the one I love and I cannot find Him. Therefore I will rise from my bed and go into vulnerable and dangerous places. My heart will reach in ways it has never reached before. I will go after the one I love." Both these dynamics are necessary; the Lord will lead us through seasons where He emphasizes the need to sit quietly and receive, and then will lead us into a place of hunger where the cry for more is awakened.

The final condition found in Proverbs 2 is seeking and searching for the Word. It describes the heart posture of one who is committed to pursuing their goal and convinced the payoff will be worth the pursuit. Proverbs 25:2 says that it is the glory of God to conceal a matter and the glory of kings to search out a matter. In other words, God intentionally hides the riches of His revelation because He knows that greater glory will be produced in our lives as we search for Him. The pursuit of God is the very thing that prepares us to receive more of Him. Seeking and searching are designed to mature us so we can bear up under the weight of revelation and encounter. God not only hides so that we will enter into greater levels of mature love; He also hides so that we will want Him more desperately and prize Him more highly. We learn to rightly value and treasure the knowledge of God when we are forced to hunt for it. Jesus declared that the kingdom of God is like treasure hidden in a field (see Matt. 13:44). When the man discovered this treasure, he sold everything in order to buy the field. Because he had invested in seeking the treasure, he was willing to sacrifice everything in order to keep it.

"If you seek her as silver, and search for her as for hidden treasures…" (Prov. 2:4). Stop and consider what it means to seek after treasure. During the 1848 California Gold Rush, thousands of people sold everything they had and traveled for weeks and months through the rough terrain of the mountains and the desert in order to find gold. Once they arrived in California, they bought the most up-to-date mining equipment and often went without sleep and food, enduring the dangers of sickness and fatigue—all for the value of the gold. Many of us are excited by the treasure but unwilling to engage in the costly work of seeking for it. Do you think those miners reached California and found piles of gold lying on the ground, waiting to be picked up? No, they had to dig for the treasure. They had to invest their time, money, and effort. The same is true for us in the Word of God. It may take months of meditating on a single verse before we receive breakthrough, but the prize is worth the investment. Colossians 2:2-3 says that all the treasures of wisdom and knowledge are hidden in Jesus. There are rubies, diamonds, and sapphires waiting to be found in the Word. If we seek the revelation of God, we will encounter treasures.

> *By night on my bed I sought the one I love; I sought him, but I did not find him. "I will rise now," I said, "and go about the city; in the streets and in the squares I will seek the one I love." I sought him, but I did not find him. The watchmen who go about the city found me; I said, "Have you seen the one I love?"* **Scarcely had I passed by them, when I found the one I love. I held him and would not let him go…** (Song of Solomon 3:1-4).

This passage illustrates the end result of a heart rightly postured before the Lord. If we carry our hearts according to the conditions of Proverbs 2, we will find the One who truly satisfies and hold on to Him tenaciously through every season of the soul.

Many of us have experienced seasons of sweet communion where our hearts grew by leaps and bounds in tenderness and sensitivity. All we had to do was blink, and we felt God's presence. But when the season changes and the old ways of encountering God aren't working, we need to awaken our spirits, rise up, and search for fresh revelation. This is the final step in preparing our hearts for meditation: we must have a seeking spirit. We must learn to hear when God is calling us to leave our comforts behind, to enter the vulnerable places of our hearts, and to wrestle with His Word until we receive breakthrough into revelation. *"I held him and would not let him go"* (Song of Sol. 3:4)—this is the fruit produced by a heart seeking after God. This is where we will end up if we take the resources given us (our time, money, and energy) and sow them into searching out the Word of God.

It is important to cultivate thankful hearts while we are in the midst of seeking after God and asking Him for more. I always want to be grateful, but I never want to be satisfied—this is a necessary kingdom tension. The breakthrough we received yesterday will eventually lead to complacency if we do not continue to press in for more. However, ingratitude for all God has done will end up imprisoning our hearts in bitterness and offense. I am grateful for everything God has done in my life—for each encounter, each moment of revelation that transformed my heart and freed my soul—but I will not let my memories of breakthrough become my plateau. I will treasure all that God has done in my life even as I arise and seek the One I love.

Chapter 6

KEYS TO MEDITATION

In the past it may have been your habit, while reading, to move very quickly from one verse of Scripture to another until you had read the whole passage. Perhaps you were seeking to find the main point of the passage. But in coming to the Lord by means of "praying the Scripture," you do not read quickly; you read very slowly. You do not move from one passage to another, not until you have sensed the very heart of what you have read. You may then want to take that portion of Scripture that has touched you and turn it into prayer. After you have sensed something of the passage and after you know that the essence of that portion has been extracted and all the deeper sense of it is gone, then, very slowly, gently, and in a calm manner begin to read the next portion of the passage. You will be surprised to find that when your time with the Lord has ended, you will have read very little, probably no more than half a page. "Praying the Scripture" is not judged by how much you read but by the way in which you read. If you read quickly, it will benefit you little.

You will be like a bee that merely skims the surface of a flower. Instead, in this new way of reading with prayer, you must become as the bee who penetrates into the depths of the flower. You plunge deeply within to remove its deepest nectar.[1]

In this chapter we will discuss a variety of tools to aid us in meditation and look at the practical steps we can take toward breakthrough in the Word of God. First, I want to examine more closely the process that led to my transforming revelation of John 17 and God's heart of desire. Many of us are aware of the moment we receive revelation from the Lord in the Word, but do not stop to think about the steps that took us there.

When I began meditating on John 17:24, I was responding to the Holy Spirit's leadership. Meditation begins with God; He draws our hearts and then we respond. Often I am led to a certain book initially, but over time my focus narrows until I am engaged with a single chapter or a verse. It is not my job to create an invitation; it is my job to enter into a verse based on the invitation of the Spirit.

The first key I stumbled upon in John 17:24 was the power of slowing down and reading the verse again and again. I simply followed the Holy Spirit and slowly, repeatedly read the passage. This helped me quiet down and rest within the Word. I believe the clearest picture of how to approach the Word of God is found in Psalm 131:1-2. *"Lord, my heart is not haughty, nor my eyes lofty. Neither do I concern myself with great matters, nor with things too profound for me. Surely I have calmed and quieted my soul, like a weaned child with his mother; like a weaned child is my soul within me."* In that place of contemplation, I began to discover other ways to engage the text: speaking phrases back to God, praying in the spirit, visualizing, and asking questions. These were not religious exercises or rigid steps that I followed. Rather, they were tools at my disposal to help me find God in the text.

I began by repeating the phrases slowly back to Him. Over time, speaking the Word out loud to God opened my heart to receive the truths contained in the passage at a deeper level. John 17:24 was no longer Jesus' prayer alone—it became my prayer: "Father, I desire to be with You where You are. I want to behold Jesus in His glory." I also discovered that lightly praying in the spirit as I read fanned the flames of love and revelation. Fellowshipping with the Holy Spirit, intermingled with sighing softly, opened my heart to increased encounter. I would pause from time to time in the midst of reading and gently exhale, allowing myself to take in the revelation. Then I began to visualize the verse. I would picture Jesus walking toward Gethsemane with the disciples and sharing the deep things of His heart. I would insert myself into the story, watching and listening as the Son asked the Father for me. Finally, I asked God questions about the things I was reading, hearing, seeing, and feeling. I let my meditation lead me into dialogue through simple questions.

This is only a brief overview of the process of meditation. Over the years I have stumbled upon a few additional tools, but the core realities I discovered in that initial season remain the same. While every individual must go on the journey of discovering how their heart engages with God in His Word, the principles behind the steps described in the preceding paragraphs apply to all believers. We are designed to receive and experience the Word of God as we engage our hearts, minds, and voices in partnership with the Holy Spirit. And one of the most effective ways of doing this is through repetition.

THE BIBLICAL DEFINITION OF MEDITATION

Blessed is the man who walks not in the counsel of the ungodly, nor stands in the path of sinners, nor sits in the seat of the scornful; but his delight is in the law of the Lord, and in His law he meditates day and night (Psalm 1:1-2).

The psalmist declared in these verses that a blessing rests upon the one who meditates on the Word of God day and night. The word *meditate* literally means "to ponder by speaking to oneself." We engage in meditation by speaking the Word to God aloud. *The verses cannot stay on the page and in our minds; they must be released through our mouths.* This is how truth is written on our hearts: we speak back to God the very things He has spoken to us.

Meditation can also be characterized as slow repetition. Just as it takes time for our bodies to break down, absorb, and digest physical food, so our spirits take time to process and receive sustenance in the Word. I like to use the eating habits of cows to illustrate meditation. A cow has four stomachs; it will eat, then regurgitate the same food, and eat it again. The food enters each of the four stomachs and is regurgitated again and again until all of the nutrients are extracted and the food is completely broken down. This is the key to assimilating the Word of God: we must stop and feel the weight of every verse, extracting the nutrition and life from each word through the process of regurgitation.

When we enter into the slow repetition of meditation, one of the first barriers we encounter is overfamiliarity with the Scriptures. It takes time to unlearn a passage in order to experience the full glory of each verse. I have found that repetition is one of the greatest ways to break down overfamiliarity and create a new vulnerability in our spirits to the power of the Word. When we slow down and begin to speak back to God the things He has spoken to us, we increasingly realize how little we know. Repetition forces us to confront the hidden pride of our hearts and the desire to move on to something new and different, something that will expand our knowledge base swiftly and effortlessly. This is why we must have a vision for breakthrough in the Word of God; without this vision, we will lack the patience and perseverance needed to push past knowledge and into revelation. Several times in the Scriptures, God commands the prophets to eat the scroll containing His words (see Ezek. 2:9-3:3; Rev. 10:8-10; Jer. 15:16). He desires a people who will do more than just read the Word. God wants us to learn how to absorb and digest the Word until it is living in us.

This is the very spirit of meditation. It is eating the same food again and again; it is wrestling with a verse until we receive breakthrough. Have you ever wrestled over something in the Word? The struggle to connect with God's heart and receive revelation creates room in our souls for the Word to abide in us. Just as Jacob was transformed when he wrestled with the Angel of the Lord (see Gen. 32:24-32), so we are simultaneously wounded and newly baptized when we refuse to move on before receiving the blessing contained in the verse before us. What does this wrestling practically look like? "I can't get breakthrough, I can't get breakthrough, I can't get breakthrough..." But I keep reading the verse over and over and over again. I keep talking to God about it and I keep listening. Then after a few weeks, specific phrases from the verse will start to jump out at me. It's like popcorn: I start a fire under a passage of Scripture and over time the kernels begin to pop one by one. I often do not realize I have been receiving impartation until that moment.

THE ROLE OF THE HOLY SPIRIT IN MEDITATION

It is common for believers to face some basic questions when they first begin to practice meditation: Where do I start? How do I know which verses to meditate on? How long should I meditate? What is the difference between studying and meditation? The answers to these questions lie in understanding the role of the Holy Spirit in the process of meditation. Have you ever noticed while reading the Bible that certain verses will sometimes stick out? It is almost as though something you have read before jumps off the page and takes on a new dimension. This happens all the time, but most of us brush past the sensation because we have to finish our reading for the day, or we only have a few minutes left before we have to move on to the next thing. We do not realize that this is actually the Holy Spirit communicating to us. He is saying, "Stop reading; I want to talk to you. Slow down. There is something for you to see here. Now say that phrase back to Me. Talk to Me about this verse."

When people ask me where they should start meditating, I often recommend the Gospel of John. I also encourage them to slow down and talk to God about what they are currently reading. As we spend time in the Word of God, the Holy Spirit will constantly highlight verses in the manner I have just described. When a verse jumps out at you or you feel a slight tug in your spirit—that inclination to take a closer look—*this is an invitation to the place of encounter.* Write the verse down and start dialoguing with God about it: "What are You saying, Lord? Why are You emphasizing this verse?"

Sometimes God will highlight more than just a verse. There have been many times when I have felt drawn to several chapters in a particular book of the Bible. Over the past decade I have frequently meditated on Romans 3-8 and the revelation of the gift of righteousness. My focus is not on a specific verse, but on experiencing deeper understanding of the doctrine contained in these chapters. As I read, God is imparting theology to my heart and teaching me about the gift of righteousness. Though I spend time unlocking each verse and letting it move me, the broader context is always in my mind. I am not trying to isolate a specific passage, but rather extracting the primary message of these five chapters.

At other times the Lord emphasizes a broader section of Scripture because He is preparing my heart before He narrows the focus of my meditation. I will keep reading the same handful of chapters for days, weeks, and even months, allowing the content to penetrate my spirit at a deeper level in spite of the fact that I may not feel much. Often I will intermingle reading with studying. For example, if I am meditating on Jeremiah, I may study the reign of Nebuchadnezzar and the timeline of Jerusalem's fall. I love commentaries; they help me understand the historical context in order to feel the weight of the words as they were originally communicated. I want to *feel* the verses in that day and apply them today. However, I generally study when my heart is already moving under the influence of the Holy Spirit. My studying benefits and guides my meditation—it adds fuel to the fire burning in my spirit by releasing additional revelation—*but I maintain the heart posture of a praying lover even as I take in new information.* Eventually the Holy Spirit will begin to highlight individual passages within those chapters, and then specific verses.

Recognizing the leadership of the Holy Spirit in this process helps me persevere until I receive breakthrough. *There are sowing and reaping seasons in the Word of God.* When I am reading chapters and verses and yet feel as though I am getting nowhere, I have learned to listen to the gentle prompting of the Spirit saying, "Plow here." I don't just want God to highlight a verse for an afternoon and give me a nice take-away point. I want to plow and wrestle and eat the scroll: "God, what are You saying? Why are You drawing me here? Speak Your Word to my heart." After a season of persevering and continuing to plow in the same verse, I will begin to reap a harvest of revelation, light, and life in my inner being. I will begin to feel the heart of God through His Word. Understanding the principle of sowing and reaping guards my heart from discouragement when I feel as though I am hitting a wall in the Bible.

We will not always sense the Holy Spirit highlighting specific chapters and verses to us. When I am not feeling led to meditate on a particular passage, I like to fill myself with the Word. There have been many periods of time when I have felt led to read ten chapters a day. God wants to expand our capacity to receive His Word, and He wants our knowledge of the Word to continually grow. It is important that we do not beat ourselves up because we are in one season as opposed to another. Recognizing that there are times when God is emphasizing width and times when He is emphasizing depth will free our hearts to respond to the leadership of the Holy Spirit. I like to say it this way: Go where there is grace. Read five to ten chapters a day, but when a verse is highlighted to you, then stop what you are doing and begin to meditate on that verse. If you feel nothing after 20 minutes or so, move on. If you can't move on for months, then stay there and keep feeding. Sometimes you may read entire books in one sitting. Other times you may hang out with a single phrase for weeks. Both are necessary—the point is to feed on the Word through regurgitation and repetition. This is how it is written on our hearts.

DEALING WITH DISTRACTION

Once you have determined to set aside time to meditate in the Word, you will inevitably run into external and internal distractions. I recommend setting aside 30 minutes to an hour each day and regarding that time as absolutely sacred. When you are first beginning, expect to be disturbed in every way possible: people you haven't heard from in years will call, the doorbell will ring, and your to-do list will yell at you. The good news is if you persevere through these distractions and remain faithful to the time you have given to God, eventually the resistance will decrease.

After you have dealt with external distractions, internal pressures will start to manifest. When you begin to read the Word of

God, for example, your mind will run in 20 different directions. This is completely normal. Most people can barely keep their thoughts focused for more than ten seconds unless they are in the midst of an intense encounter with the Holy Spirit. Saint Teresa of Avila described this phenomenon, saying it felt as though a frantic madman was running around inside her head.[2] What you must learn to do is bring your mind back to God without condemning yourself. After your thoughts have run their course, simply focus again on the verse before you. If you develop the habit of turning your thoughts back to God, over time your ability to focus will increase.

A significant portion of our mental traffic is related to tasks. When we begin to dial down, everything we need to accomplish (paying bills, making phone calls, and running errands) will come rushing to the surface of our thoughts. Many people find it helpful to keep a piece of paper nearby so they can write these things down as they come to mind. Writing down everything you need to do not only helps you remember it later, but also allows your mind to relax and refocus on God.

Another distraction can come in the form of studying. Meditating on a specific verse can trigger all sorts of ideas about word studies we want to complete and other passages we want to cross-reference. We can easily end up fruitlessly skipping around from verse to verse. I would encourage you to keep a list of topics you want to explore at a later point. Meditation is the discipline of feeding yourself on individual verses. Write down your ideas for future studies, and then return your thoughts to the words in front of you.

We are commanded to pray without ceasing (see 1 Thess. 5:17). One of the ways we can do this is by turning our thoughts into prayers. When you are trying to read the Word but find yourself thinking about friends and family, begin to pray for them. If you are worrying about a situation at work, invite the Lord to speak to you about it. This is one way to transform your wandering thoughts into communion with God. Remember that when it comes to meditation in the Word, you are not trying to empty your mind—that is Eastern mysticism. The goal in meditation is to fill your mind with the Word of God and to captivate your thought-life with the revelation of God. And don't forget to ask the Holy Spirit for help. The Spirit loves to give us grace to encounter God in His Word.

BREAKING THE WORD INTO PHRASES

> It is not necessary that we should get through the entire passage in one meditation. Often we shall have to stop with one sentence or even one word, because we have been gripped and arrested and cannot evade it any longer. Is not the word "Father," or "love," "mercy," "cross," "sanctification," "resurrection," often enough to fill far more than the brief period at our disposal?[3]

One of the most significant things I learned through meditating on Psalm 119 is the power of breaking the Word into short phrases. As I mentioned in Chapter 4, this psalm is written in couplets—each verse is comprised of two rhyming lines which communicate a complete thought. Reading through Psalm 119 taught me to slow down, stop after each phrase, and dialogue with God. Small phrases are easier to mentally digest and connect with emotionally. When I focus in on a sentence or phrase, I like to use a highlighter and pen. Writing down the things that I hear God speaking and circling the words that stand out help me to remain focused on the verse. Small phrases need to become our feeding ground in the Word. The longer we remain there, the more we will uncover. Through individual words, God often reminds me of other passages in the Bible that relate to my meditation. I then use my pen to add these verses to the present passage. Over time a theme usually develops inside of me and I begin to be caught up in the Word.

VISUALIZATION AND DIALOGUE

Words create images—that is one of the reasons they are so powerful. We are all familiar with the same Gospel narratives, but we have different ideas of how the stories unfolded. When we read about Jesus feeding the 5,000, you may picture Him at the base of a gently sloping hill while I may see Him seated halfway up a mountain. Everyone creates their own images based on the words they read. The truth is that we are designed to experience life visually and imaginatively. God wants access to the creativity of our minds. He is an artist who wants to paint reality on our hearts and in our lives.

> *But we all, with unveiled face, beholding as in a mirror the glory of the Lord, are being transformed into the same image from glory to glory, just as by the Spirit of the Lord* (2 Corinthians 3:18).

According to the apostle Paul, we are created to be transformed by what we look at. The pictures invoked in our mind's eye when we read the Bible open us up to receive more from God. When I am meditating on a passage of Scripture, I engage my imagination and let the images draw me into an encounter with the Word. For example, if I am reading John 17, I will start at the beginning of the chapter and slowly read until I feel the Holy Spirit begin to breathe on a verse. Then I will slow down even more and linger over each phrase as I begin to fix my mind's eye on the story unfolding before me. I may pause to meditate on John 17:5, *"And now, O Father, glorify Me together with Yourself, with the glory which I had with You before the world was."* As I focus on specific phrases within this verse, I am invited to gaze on the eternity of God and the pre-existence of Jesus. I envision the throne room and countless angels worshiping the Father and the Son before the foundations of the world were laid. The Holy Spirit is painting a picture for me to experience, and as I enter into the divine invitation, I become a participant in the story. It is no longer only the apostle John's encounter; I am able to listen to Jesus speak to His Father about the glory they shared in eternity past. This is a practical way to engage the spirit of revelation. Although John wrote these words over 2,000 years ago, they are still alive and we are invited to see God through them.

> Love desires to have the beloved before its eyes. Thus the contemplative will employ the powers of his soul to summon up the image of the Beloved, the powers of his "inner senses" and his imagination to call forth the image of the incarnate Word. He will contemplate Jesus as he dwelt bodily on the earth, the things he said, the sound of his voice, the way he treated people, his appearance when at prayer, at the Last Supper, in his Passion. This picture is not meant to be a realistic photograph, but love's picture, solely concerned with love, the divine love of the Father, which is here manifested in the Son and in the concreteness of his whole earthly life.[4]

Not only do I fix the eyes of my heart on the pictures of God in the verses before me, but I also talk to the Holy Spirit as I read. I have found that it is helpful to speak to Him aloud, but I keep my voice quiet in order to preserve the sense of intimacy. I repeat the phrases that are drawing me into meditation, and I ask for greater revelation. Through engaging my imagination and dialoguing with the Spirit, I am able to enter into the Word. I find myself in the story and hear the Word of God speaking to me today. When that happens, revelation begins to flow. I may hear a few phrases of a message or be reminded of other verses that connect to the theme of my meditation. Some people receive songs or poems. Regardless of what form the revelation takes, it is accompanied by the sensation of a burning heart.

I don't want you to have an overly idealized expectation when it comes to receiving revelation. It is true that our hearts are impacted whenever God speaks to us through His Word, but often it takes time for that revelation to conquer our hearts. "You like me?" This is how we feel when we begin to meditate on the love of God: 99 percent of our heart thinks God is distant, disappointed, and disinterested, while 1 percent believes that He likes us. As we continue to meditate on Scripture and speak the truth back to God—"You like me"—the spirit of revelation is released and those percentages start changing. Suddenly 2 percent of our heart is convinced that God loves us and only 98 percent is skeptical. It might take six months or even a few years, but if we faithfully continue to talk to God through the Word, we will grow in the experiential knowledge of the truth.

> To receive any deep, inward profit from the Scripture you must read as I have described. Plunge into the very depths of the words you read until revelation, like a sweet aroma, breaks out upon you.[5]

THE POWER OF ASKING QUESTIONS

One of the greatest keys to dialoguing with God in the Word is asking questions. Too often if we hear a verse or receive a little revelation, our response is, "Oh, that was nice." We are mistaking an invitation for a conclusion. God shows us a little because He wants us to ask for more. The power to move into the Word at a deeper level comes through asking questions. When a verse or phrase hits you, write it down and inquire: "What is going on? What are You saying, Holy Spirit?" We must learn how to lock in on a verse through slow repetition and questions.

Have you ever wondered why God asks questions? In Ezekiel 37:3 God speaks to the prophet and says, *"Son of man, can these bones live?"* God is not asking because He needs an answer. In fact, Ezekiel responds by saying, *"O Lord God, You know."* In other words, "Don't ask me." The reason God asked the question was to invite Ezekiel into the spirit of prophecy. The question is an invitation. God asked, *"Jeremiah, what do you see?"* *"I see a branch of an almond tree,"* he replied (Jer. 1:11). God did not need the aid of Jeremiah's eyes; He was ushering Jeremiah into the prophetic spirit. He wants us to see what He sees and hear what He hears. *The questions are an invitation into deeper communication and understanding.*

The same is true when we ask God questions. We can enter into revelation and engage the prophetic spirit by asking questions as we read the Word. When God begins to highlight phrases to me, I have a set of questions I like to ask: Who? What? Where? When? Why? How? These five questions bring me into the spirit of revelation. God loves to answer these questions. For example, in John 17:26 Jesus continues to pray to the Father on our behalf and reveal all that He desires to release in our lives: *"And I have declared to them Your name, and will declare it, that the love with which You loved Me may be in them, and I in them."* I might start by asking, "Jesus, *how* did You declare the name of the Father? In *what* ways did Your words and actions reveal God's name? *Why* did You choose to reveal the nature of Your Father to me?" Wrestling over these questions will begin to form prayers within me: "Jesus, come and declare the Father's name to me. I want to know Him just as You know Him." I engage Jesus through the Word as I ask Him to show me more and take me further into the story, into the reality of God's love.

THE POWER OF SINGING THE WORD

Singing is another powerful way to get the Word of God inside your soul. A friend of mine once asked Mike Bickle what

EATING THE SCROLL

…God sends his spokesmen, and these are always men who have themselves heard the word individually, whose ability to hear has been tested in the school of solitude, like Moses and Ezekiel (Ezek 3:24). Solitaries such as these often groan under the burden of the word which they have to proclaim to a stiff-necked people that does not want to hear; they yearn for a simple life; yet it would never occur to them to shirk being involved in the people's destiny. Hearing the word never takes place simply for the personal satisfaction of hearing it; it is always directed to a common obedience.[1]

Jeremiah was a solitary man. In the midst of a generation that had hardened their hearts and stopped their ears, he heard the voice of the Lord and responded. He became the messenger God used to call His people back to the ancient paths, to the place of hearing. The religious leaders of the day had no intimacy with the Word and therefore gave the wrong interpretation of the hour. They promised peace and prosperity when judgment was at the door. The Lord warned the people through Jeremiah that their discernment had become worthless because they were listening to the wrong message:

> *Thus says the Lord of hosts: "Do not listen to the words of the prophets who prophesy to you. They make you worthless; they speak a vision of their own heart, not from the mouth of the Lord. They continually say to those who despise Me, 'The Lord has said, "You shall have peace"'; And to everyone who walks according to the dictates of his own heart, they say, 'No evil shall come upon you'"* (Jeremiah 23:16-17).

We are experiencing the same crisis today. Though there are many churches, pulpits, and media platforms releasing Christian messages, the Word of the Lord is scarce. In verse 18 Jeremiah cried out, *"For who has stood in the counsel of the Lord, and has perceived and heard His word? Who has marked His word and heard it?"* This is the core question facing our generation: Who is truly hearing from God? Who has engaged in long and loving meditation on the Word and entered into the counsel of the Lord?

A few verses later, Jeremiah revealed that one of the fundamental differences between true and false prophets is impatience. True prophets wait on the Lord, while false prophets run ahead before they are sent (see Jer. 23:21-22). Something takes place in our souls as we spend time waiting before the Word. We are gradually delivered from the need to speak what others want to hear, and the fear of man is replaced by the fear of the Lord.

Paul warned Timothy that in the last days people would cease to listen to truth. Instead, they would run after every word that tickled their ears and promoted their personal comfort:

> *For the time will come when they will not endure sound doctrine, but according to their own desires, because they have itching ears, they will heap up for themselves teachers; and they*

will turn their ears away from the truth, and be turned aside to fables (2 Timothy 4:3-4).

If we want to hear and rightly discern what the Spirit is saying to the church today, we must train our spiritual ears through long and loving meditation in the Word.

The hour is late, and God is calling people to stand in His counsel, allowing the Word to penetrate and transform them. He is marking a generation with devotion to the Scriptures; their lives will be consumed with holy fire, and they will come forth with clarity, authority, and anointing in the greatest hour of human history. The words they speak will emerge from the Word they have become. The ultimate purpose of the Word is to become flesh.

When the people asked John the Baptist who he was, he quoted the prophet Isaiah: "I am the voice of one crying in the wilderness" (John 1:23 paraphrased). He had read Isaiah 40 so many times that he became Isaiah 40. The message of the coming Messiah was not just something John prophesied; it was something he embodied. When God desired to announce the coming of His Son, He entrusted the message to a man in the wilderness, a man who had stood in His counsel.

Today, God desires to manifest His Word in and through us. He is preparing end-time messengers—men and women who will be fashioned and formed through decades of prayer, fasting, and meditation in the Word. In Matthew 11:9 Jesus declared that John the Baptist was more than a prophet. I believe that God is raising up people who will be more than what they say; their very lives will prophesy the changing of the seasons. And in the same way John was prepared in the wilderness before the first coming of the Christ, so the Lord will prepare these end-time messengers in the wilderness of prayer and meditation.

THE ROLE OF THE WILDERNESS

Throughout the Bible we see that God chooses again and again to form His people in the wilderness. It is the furnace of transformation; the place where our facades, illusions, fantasies, and props are removed and we come face to face with our nothingness. In the wilderness God strips us of our independence and rebellion and teaches us to depend on Him and embrace a life of sacrifice and leaning. The end of the Song of Solomon describes the bride coming out of the wilderness leaning on her beloved (see Song of Sol. 8:5). This is the place where we discover His strength is made perfect in our weakness.

"Therefore, behold, I will allure her, will bring her into the wilderness, and speak comfort to her" (Hos. 2:14). In the beginning of our journey, the Word of God allures us. We experience the pleasure of God's love—He thrills our hearts and tenderizes our souls with His sweet presence. This love breaks down our defenses and walls, making us susceptible to the Word at a deeper level. "I love Your Word. Kiss me with the kisses of Your Word, cleanse me, wash me, renew me, set me on fire, break the rock into pieces." As we make these declarations, the sweetness of the Word overcomes our resistance and positions our heart for transformation. But this is just the beginning.

After He allures us, God leads us into the wilderness. This is the place where we begin swimming against the current of our culture and spending our time, energy, and resources on prayer, fasting, and meditation in the Word. Often our first experience in this new season is a feeling of restlessness and loneliness. Many of us have never really been quiet before—we have never disconnected from the things that prop up our lives and distract us from the true state of our hearts. We are always surrounded by our family, friends, work, music, entertainment, etc. But once we take a step back from these things in order to feed on the Word, we begin to encounter our own barrenness.

Have you ever seen an addict go through detox? This is how I picture the experience of the wilderness. Our society has trained us to medicate our pain with noise, entertainment, and distraction. If we want to hear what God is saying in His Word, we must embrace the wilderness and withdraw from these addictions of the soul until we are actually quiet on the inside. The Lord wants to speak to us, but first we must become a people who have dialed down so we can receive His voice and experience His transformational work in our hearts. In the season of the wilderness, God says, "I have drawn you away and set you in a furnace, and now I want to quiet you and begin to speak tenderly to your heart."

Many times throughout the Scriptures we find this motif the *wilderness*. If we pursue a life of meditation, eventually God will bring us to a place—not a geographical wilderness, but a place within our hearts—where we are forced to surrender everything else we are living on.

> *And you shall remember that the Lord your God led you all the way these forty years in the wilderness, to humble you and test you, to know what was in your heart, whether you would keep His commandments or not. So He humbled you, allowed you to hunger, and fed you with manna which you did not know nor did your fathers know, that He might make you know that man shall not live by bread alone; but man lives by every word that proceeds from the mouth of the Lord* (Deuteronomy 8:2-3).

Have you ever wondered why God led Israel through the desert before allowing them to enter the Promised Land? After He took them out of Egypt, He needed to take Egypt out of them. Look at what it says: *"He humbled you,* [He] *allowed you to hunger..."* God created a context that caused them to starve and reach and confront their weakness. He allowed it; He stood back and said, "Now what are you going to do here?" He tested their hearts to see whether they would continue to follow Him when it cost them their comfort and security. But when they reached for God in the place of hunger and need, He sent heavenly manna.

The word *manna* literally means "what is it?" When we encounter the Word of God, it exposes our false expectations and secret idols. The generation of Israelites that died in the wilderness preferred slavery to dependence on God. "We would rather be slaves and have stability than live as free men and look to God to meet our every need. We would rather submit to harsh taskmasters who provide us with familiar food than rely on the Word of God to sustain us." According to this passage in Deuteronomy, God sent Israel manna so that they would learn their lives depended on His Word: "He caused you to know that man shall not live by bread alone, but by every word that proceeds from the mouth of the Lord" (Deut. 8:3b paraphrased).

THE PROGRESSION FROM DELIGHTING TO TREMBLING

Many years ago I received a powerful prophetic word from a relatively unknown person. I was told the Lord had made Psalm 119 my foundation, but that He was taking me into the reality of Isaiah 66:2: *"But on this one will I look: on him who is poor and of a contrite spirit, and who trembles at My word."* Psalm 119 speaks of delighting in the Word—it is the foundation of love, intimacy, and joy—while Isaiah 66 describes a heart that trembles before the Word in reverent fear.

I believe this is the progression of a messenger: we receive the Word with delight, but as it works within us, it begins to produce a holy trembling. Though we never leave the place of holy enjoyment and pleasure, if we seek to mature, we must learn to bring every area of our life underneath the leadership of the Word.

> *He who rejects Me, and does not receive My words, has that which judges him—the word that I have spoken will judge him in the last day* (John 12:48).

Jesus stated that we will be judged based on our ability to hear and respond rightly. This reality confronts our tendency to approach the Word as a set of flexible guidelines meant to primarily serve our comfort and convenience. But there is coming a day when the Word of God will be declared over us and our lives will be evaluated based on whether or not we submitted to it. In light of this truth, our greatest safety is found in becoming vulnerable to the Word, asking for a holy trembling and the gift of humility as we seek to encounter God in our meditation. I want His Word to judge me now instead of judging me on that day. I do not want to stand on the edge of eternity and be shocked by how little of my life has survived the judgment of the Word.

Hearing must produce an active obedience. God desires our hearts to be responsive. *"If you love Me, keep My commandments,"* Jesus said (John 14:15). *"For this is the love of God, that we keep His commandments"* (1 John 5:3a). We declare our love for Jesus by our obedience to His commandments. Obedience is the sincere desire to do what Jesus calls us to do, and the maturing ability to respond to His commands. We must cultivate obedience by posturing our hearts in humility before the Word.

> If we fail to let the word's sharp edge have its effect on us, we shall always be meeting a merely imaginary Redeemer; if we fail to face the judgment of Christ every time we contemplate, we shall not perceive the distinctive quality of divine grace. The consuming fire of crucified Love is both redemption and judgment; the two are inseparable and indistinguishable.

It almost does not matter which word of holy scripture the contemplative chooses; the fire to which he exposes himself will not abate until it has penetrated his inmost being, provided that he yields to it and does not draw back.[2]

When we tremble before the Word of God, it is not a place of torment. Rather, it is the recognition that God's Word has a claim on us and we owe it everything. Trembling simply means that God's voice is stronger and louder than every other voice. The one who trembles has come underneath the power of the Word. They not only experience delight in the Scriptures, but all they read and hear moves them to obedience. Many of us stop at the experience of delight and never enter into the place of trembling, the place where the Word of God owns us.

Your words were found, and I ate them, and Your word was to me the joy and rejoicing of my heart.... I sat alone because of Your hand, for You have filled me with indignation. Why is my pain perpetual and my wound incurable, which refuses to be healed? (Jeremiah 15:16-18)

Jeremiah declared that the Word of God was the joy of his heart. His initial encounters with the Word filled him with delight and rejoicing. But over time that same Word produced a trembling obedience and radical allegiance within him—an allegiance which sparked great opposition and enmity in those around him, including his own family. We see this pattern again and again in the lives of those called to speak the Word of God with power and authority to their generation. God allures His messengers with tenderness, love, and delight into the wilderness where He causes them to eat His Word and count the cost of obedience and discipleship.

In addition to this passage in Jeremiah, we find two other accounts in the Bible where an individual is commanded to "eat" the Word of God.

"But you, son of man, hear what I say to you. Do not be rebellious like that rebellious house; open your mouth and eat what I give you."

Now when I looked, there was a hand stretched out to me; and behold, a scroll of a book was in it. Then He spread it before me; and there was writing on the inside and on the outside, and written on it were lamentations and mourning and woe.

Moreover He said to me, **"Son of man, eat what you find; eat this scroll, and go, speak to the house of Israel." So I opened my mouth, and He caused me to eat that scroll.**

And He said to me, "Son of man, feed your belly, and fill your stomach with this scroll that I give you." **So I ate, and it was in my mouth like honey in sweetness** (Ezekiel 2:8–3:3).

In this passage the scroll represents the specific prophetic oracles intended for Ezekiel's generation, but it also refers to the whole of the Torah. Notice that though the scroll contained lamentations and woe, it was sweet like honey to the taste. In the midst of an encounter related to judgment, Ezekiel experienced the delight of the Word. The sweetness was a reminder that God is good and His judgments flow from His heart as a Bridegroom. In Jeremiah 2:2, before the destruction of Jerusalem, God declared that He remembered the kindness of the nation's youth and the love of their betrothal. This is what was on His mind as He prepared to release judgment. The crisis of Israel's rebellion in Ezekiel's day demanded a response, but that response came from a God of love committed to restoring His people to Himself at all costs. Ezekiel was equipped to communicate this message because he experienced it as he ate the Word. The scroll was both bitter and sweet.

In the New Testament, John had a similar experience during his Revelation encounter.

I saw still another mighty angel coming down from heaven, clothed with a cloud. And a rainbow was on his head, his face was like the sun, and his feet like pillars of fire. He had a little book open in his hand. And he set his right foot on the sea and his left foot on the land, and cried with a loud voice, as when a lion roars. When he cried out, seven thunders uttered their voices....

Then the voice which I heard from heaven spoke to me again and said, "Go, take the little book which is open in the hand of the angel who stands on the sea and on the earth."

So I went to the angel and said to him, "Give me the little book."

*And he said to me, **"Take and eat it; and it will make your stomach bitter, but it will be as sweet as honey in your mouth."***

***Then I took the little book out of the angel's hand and ate it, and it was as sweet as honey in my mouth. But when I had eaten it, my stomach became bitter.** And he said to me, "You must prophesy again about many peoples, nations, tongues, and kings"* (Revelation 10:1-3;8-11).

Again we see the progression of the Word of God in the life of a messenger. As John eats the book, he experiences its sweetness, delight, and pleasure. However, the book is a prophetic oracle concerning the end times; it communicates God's zeal and commitment to utterly eradicate sin from the earth. The judgments described in Revelation are bitter, and John literally feels the conflict between the kingdoms of heaven and hell as his stomach churns. But just as John the Baptist became the voice of one crying in the wilderness through his experience of the Word in the wilderness, so John the Beloved became the messenger of the second coming through his experience of the Word's bitter and sweet truths.

I believe that God is going to call forth revivalists and preachers who will not pick their favorite passages while ignoring everything else in the Bible. They will not focus on the easy, comfortable, and happy messages alone; they will eat the whole book. In Exodus, God commands Israel to eat the entire Passover lamb and not let any of it remain until morning (see Exod. 12:3-10). This same command applies to us today, but many parts of the lamb are left untouched. This is where the transformation of the wilderness will manifest in our lives: we will stop choosing our messages and begin to speak whatever He commands us. In Revelation 10 the angel told John that he *must* prophesy—in other words, there is a constraint on the messenger. They are not dictating the content but are constrained to say what God is saying. They have taken the time to eat the Word—not just read it, but eat and digest it—and are now living in unity with that Word.

THE REVELATION OF JESUS CHRIST

In these last days there are going to be many books of the Bible that God will cause His messengers to eat, but I believe the book of Revelation will be the most emphasized and necessary of all. The popular teaching on the end times has left the church believing the truths contained in Revelation are irrelevant. Most of us have avoided the subject of eschatology, leaving it to academics and theologians. We have stuck our heads in the sand and said, "The content is too difficult to understand, and it will all work out eventually, so why bother?" However, this book contains more insight into the nature, heart, and plans of Jesus than any other book in the Bible. It is called *The Revelation of Jesus Christ*—it is not the revelation of Satan, the antichrist, or the judgment of humanity. The glory, majesty, and power of Jesus as He redeems the earth are on full display in this book. We see in remarkable detail His plan to release justice in the nations, establish His reign on earth, and bring His Father's house to Jerusalem. We also see a church, free from offense, in full agreement with His leadership, and partnering with the songs of heaven that release the final judgments.

Few of us realize that there is a blessing given to those who read Revelation: *"Blessed is he who reads and those who hear the words of this prophecy, and keep those things which are written in it; for the time is near"* (Rev. 1:3). Nowhere else in the Scriptures is a blessing promised to those who read the Word. Think about this: Who in their right mind would begin reading a novel, reach the climax, and then shut the book? When the king's wife has been abducted by the villain and the king is preparing to rescue her, do we say, "Well, I know what's going to happen: the king is going to defeat the villain and save his wife. Why bother reading the end?" No! We want to read the end of the story for ourselves. Yet the body of Christ has shut the Bible at the climax of human history. Revelation contains the end of our story; it is the ultimate drama of human history. We need to be connected to this story. It is not too difficult to understand—it was written for unlearned, uneducated people. It means what it says and it says what it means. We all qualify as people who can read, hear, and understand this book.[3]

When the disciples asked Jesus what the sign of His coming would be at the end of the age, He gave them a list of conditions— some political, some geophysical, and some spiritual—that would indicate His return. This list included ethnic strife, conflict on a global scale, famines and earthquakes, a great falling away, and the proclamation of the gospel to the ends of the earth (see Matt. 24:3-13). Jesus then stated He would return *after* the list of conditions was fulfilled (see Matt. 24:29-30).

We live in a unique period of human history. Israel is back in the land after 2,000 years of exile, leaders of prominent missions organizations agree that we are less than a decade away from seeing the fulfillment of the Great Commission, and everywhere we look, international crises and conflicts seem to be on the rise. For all these reasons, I believe it is time we begin to read the book of Revelation.

The final years before the second coming, commonly known as the Great Tribulation, will be the church's finest hour—but we will only be prepared for those years to the extent that we meditate on the truths contained in Revelation. This is the only way we will begin to understand the heart of God as He orchestrates the glorious and terrifying events which will purify His people and destroy the antichrist along with every hostile ruler and nation. Though there are many who teach that the church will be gone during the most intense period of judgment, I do not believe this view is consistent with the nature of God and the witness of Scripture. I encourage you to ask God to reveal His heart and His plans to you as you read and meditate upon end-time prophecy. The book of Revelation was written for you.

CLOSING THOUGHTS

The words of Jeremiah are echoing today across the Earth: "Stand in the ways, and ask for the ancient paths" (Jer. 6:16a paraphrased). I long to see a generation arise that has spent decades at the feet of Jesus, allowing the Word of God to consume them and be made manifest in them until their voices, united with the Word, break the prophetic silence all over the earth. I plead with you, dear reader, to take your place at His feet, ask Him for a revival in the Bible, and begin your journey of meditation. He will blow your mind…

ENDNOTES

Chapter 1: Ancient Paths

1. For the full narrative see Second Kings 18-19.

2. Arthur Katz, Paul Volk, *The Spirit of Truth* (Charlotte: MorningStar Publications, 1993), 16.

3. Jono Hall, Allen Hood, Stephen Venable, "Is the Bible Authoritative? IHOPU Faculty Discusses...," YouTube, http://www.youtube.com/watch?v=dmP-L-mMjCg (accessed February 8, 2012).

4. Stephen Charnock, "Discourse II: On Practical Atheism," in *Discourses upon the Existence and Attributes of God* (New York: Robert Carter & Brothers, 1874), 89, under http://books.google.com/books?id=NtZJAAA AMAAJ&printsec=frontcover&dq=discourses+upo n+the+existence+and+attributes+of+God&hl=en&sa =X&ei=erQT9SRGrSs0AH09PTjDQ&ved=0CDg Q6AEwAA#v=onepage&q=discourses%20upon%20

the%20existence%20and%20attributes%20of%20
God&f=false (accessed February 15, 2012).

5. Hans Urs von Balthasar, along with the other Catholic
    writers and mystics quoted in this book, should be read
    with caution. While I do not agree with all of his theo-
    logical positions, I do believe that the content I have
    chosen to highlight in this book carries valuable spiri-
    tual truths.

6. Hans Urs von Balthasar, *Prayer*, trans. Graham Har-
    rison (San Francisco: Ignatius Press, 1986), 16.

7. A. W. Tozer, *The Knowledge of the Holy* (New York:
    HarperOne, 1961), vii.

8. Thomas Merton, trans., *The Wisdom of the Desert:
    Sayings from the Desert Fathers of the Fourth Century*
    (Boston: Shambhala Publications, Inc., 2004), 1-2.

9. Henri Nouwen, *The Way of the Heart: Desert Spiritual-
    ity and Contemporary Ministry* (New York: HarperOne,
    1981), 14.

10. Hans Urs von Balthasar, *Prayer*, trans. Graham Har-
    rison (San Francisco: Ignatius Press, 1986), 15.

11. See Isaiah 55:1-3, Jeremiah 2:13, and John 4:10-13.

Chapter 2: Jesus the Word

1. Henri Nouwen, The Way of the Heart: Desert Spiri-
    tuality and Contemporary Ministry (New York:
    HarperOne, 1981), 48.

2. Henri Nouwen, The Way of the Heart: Desert Spiri-
    tuality and Contemporary Ministry (New York:
    HarperOne, 1981), 45-46.

3. Hans Urs von Balthasar, Prayer, trans. Graham Harrison (San Francisco: Ignatius Press, 1986), 15.

4. David Baron, Zechariah: A Commentary on His Visions and Prophecies (Grand Rapids: Kregel Publications), 23.

5. Hans Urs von Balthasar, Prayer, trans. Graham Harrison (San Francisco: Ignatius Press, 1986), 164.

Chapter 3: The Call to Hear

1. Hans Urs von Balthasar, *Prayer*, trans. Graham Harrison (San Francisco: Ignatius Press, 1986), 18-19.

2. New Testament passages where this is proclaimed are Mark 4:9; Luke 8:8; 14:35; Matthew 11:15; 13:9,43; Revelation 2:7,11,17,29; 3:6,13,22; and 13:9.

3. Bob Sorge, *In His Face* (Greenwood, MO: Oasis House, 1994), 54.

4. Hans Urs von Balthasar, *Prayer*, trans. Graham Harrison (San Francisco: Ignatius Press, 1986), 22.

Chapter 4: Delighting in the Word

1. Many scholars agree that David is the probable author of Psalm 119 based on similarities in content and style between this psalm and his other psalms. Charles Spurgeon, in his commentary on the book of Psalms, supports this conclusion and lays out his arguments in favor of attributing Davidic authorship. See *The Treasury of David*, Volume VI, if you are interested in more information.

2. Watson E. Mills, Richard F. Vilson, eds., *History of Israel*, vol. 2 of *The Mercer Commentary on the Bible* (Macon: Mercer University Press, 1999), 111.

3. C. H. Spurgeon, *Psalms 90-150*, vol. 2 of *The Treasury of David: An Expository and Devotional Commentary on the Psalms* (Grand Rapids: Baker Book House, 1984), vi.

4. C. H. Spurgeon, *Psalms 90-150*, vol. 2 of *The Treasury of David: An Expository and Devotional Commentary on the Psalms* (Grand Rapids: Baker Book House, 1984), 1.

5. Matthew Henry, *An Account of the Life and Death of Mr. Philip Henry, Minister of the Gospel, Near Whitechurch in Shropshire* (London: Printed for J. Lawrence, 1712), 168, under http://openlibrary.org/books/OL20454300M/An_Account_of_the_Life_and_Death_of_Mr._Philip_Henry_Minister_of_the_Gospel_Near_Whitchurch_in_... (accessed April 18, 2012).

6. Paul Bond, "Film Industry, Led By Electronic Delivery, Will Grow in Every Category Through 2015: Report (Exclusive)," *The Hollywood Reporter,* June 14, 2011, under http://www.hollywoodreporter.com/news/film-industry-led-by-electronic-200881 (accessed April 16, 2012).

7. Ben Woolsey, Matt Schulz, eds., "Credit card statistics, industry facts, debt statistics," in CreditCards.com, http://www.creditcards.com/credit-card-news/credit-card-industry-facts-personal-debt-statistics-1276.php#footnote1 (accessed April 17, 2012).

8. Thomas Dubay, *Fire Within* (San Francisco: Ignatius Press, 1989), 139.

9. St. Augustine, *The Confessions of St. Augustine*, ed. Rosalie De Rosset, (Chicago: Moody Publishers, 2007), 19.

10. Hans Urs von Balthasar, *Prayer*, trans. Graham Harrison (San Francisco: Ignatius Press, 1986), 130.

11. C. H. Spurgeon, *Psalms 90-150*, vol. 2 of *The Treasury of David: An Expository and Devotional Commentary on the Psalms* (Grand Rapids: Baker Book House, 1984), 11.

12. C. H. Spurgeon, *Psalms 90-150*, vol. 2 of *The Treasury of David: An Expository and Devotional Commentary on the Psalms* (Grand Rapids: Baker Book House, 1984), 15.

13. C. H. Spurgeon, *Psalms 90-150*, vol. 2 of *The Treasury of David: An Expository and Devotional Commentary on the Psalms* (Grand Rapids: Baker Book House, 1984), 73-74.

14. C. H. Spurgeon, *Psalms 90-150*, vol. 2 of *The Treasury of David: An Expository and Devotional Commentary on the Psalms* (Grand Rapids: Baker Book House, 1984), 166.

15. C. H. Spurgeon, *Psalms 90-150*, vol. 2 of *The Treasury of David: An Expository and Devotional Commentary on the Psalms* (Grand Rapids: Baker Book House, 1984), 130.

Chapter 5: Breaking Through the Pages

1. Mike Bickle, "How to Encounter Jesus as the Son of Man," session 7 of *Jesus Our Magnificent Obsession* (sermon presented at the IHOP Encounter God Service on October 28, 2011).

2. Hans Urs von Balthasar, *Prayer*, trans. Graham Harrison (San Francisco: Ignatius Press, 1986), 91.

Chapter 6: Keys to Meditation

1. Jeanne Guyon, *Experiencing the Depths of Jesus Christ*, vol. 2 of *Library of Spiritual Classics* (Sargent: SeedSowers Christian Books Publishing House, 1975), 7-8.

2. *Teresa of Avila: The book of her life*, trans. Kieran Kavanaugh and Otilio Rodriguez (Indianapolis: Hackett Publishing Company, 2008), 209.

3. Dietrich Bonhoeffer, *Life Together: The Classic Exploration of Faith in Community* (San Francisco: Harper & Row Publishers Inc., 1954), 83.

4. Hans Urs von Balthasar, *Prayer*, trans. Graham Harrison (San Francisco: Ignatius Press, 1986), 129.

5. Jeanne Guyon, *Experiencing the Depths of Jesus Christ*, vol. 2 of *Library of Spiritual Classics* (Sargent: SeedSowers Christian Books Publishing House, 1975), 8.

6. Mike Bickle has written an excellent book on fasting: *The Rewards of Fasting*. I highly recommend this book for those interested in learning more about the biblical basis and spiritual benefits of fasting. It also contains practical tips designed to help the reader maintain physical health while pursuing a lifestyle of regular fasting.

7. Henri Nouwen, *The Way of the Heart: Desert Spirituality and Contemporary Ministry* (New York: HarperOne, 1981), 82-83.

Chapter 7: One Thing Needed

1. Dietrich Bonhoeffer, *Life Together: The Classic Exploration of Faith in Community* (San Francisco: Harper & Row Publishers Inc., 1954), 84.

2. Robert E. Picirilli, *The Gospel of Mark*, The Randall House Bible Commentary (Nashville: Randall House Publications, 2003), 374.

Chapter 8: Tearing Down Strongholds

1. Hans Urs von Balthasar, *Prayer*, trans. Graham Harrison (San Francisco: Ignatius Press, 1986), 234.

2. Strongholds are not only demonic. Many times in the Scriptures we read that God is our stronghold, a tower of strength and resource. Simply put, a stronghold is the system of beliefs and way of life we cling to in the face of pressure. God desires to tear down strongholds of darkness and build up strongholds of truth within us. *"The name of the Lord is a strong tower; the righteous run to it and are safe"* (Prov. 18:10).

Chapter 9: Eating the Scroll

1. Hans Urs von Balthasar, *Prayer*, trans. Graham Harrison (San Francisco: Ignatius Press, 1986), 86.

2. Hans Urs von Balthasar, *Prayer*, trans. Graham Harrison (San Francisco: Ignatius Press, 1986), 224-225.

3. For a practical and accessible introductory study of the book of Revelation, I highly recommend Mike Bickle's *Book of Revelation Study Guide*.

ABOUT THE AUTHOR

Corey Russell has served on the senior leadership team of the International House of Prayer (IHOP-KC) for the last 12 years. He is the Director of the Forerunner Program at the International House of Prayer University (IHOPU), discipling and training young preachers and leaders. He travels nationally and internationally, preaching on the themes of the Knowledge of God, Intercession, and the Forerunner Ministry. He resides in Kansas City with his wife, Dana, and their four children: Trinity, Mya, Hadassah, and Nash.

For booking and tracking with Corey's ministry:

www.coreyrussell.org.

Follow Corey on Twitter: @BrotherRussell

Follow Corey on Facebook: Official CoreyRussell

OTHER RESOURCES BY COREY RUSSELL

Pursuit of the Holy

Eyes Opened (CD)

Ancient Paths (CD)

IN THE RIGHT HANDS, THIS BOOK WILL CHANGE LIVES!

Most of the people who need this message will not be looking for this book. To change their lives, you need to put a copy of this book in their hands.

> *But others (seeds) fell into good ground, and brought forth fruit, some a hundred-fold, some sixty-fold, some thirty-fold* (Matthew 13:8).

Our ministry is constantly seeking methods to find the good ground, the people who need this anointed message to change their lives. Will you help us reach these people?

> *Remember this—a farmer who plants only a few seeds will get a small crop. But the one who plants generously will get a generous crop* (2 Corinthians 9:6).

EXTEND THIS MINISTRY BY SOWING
3 BOOKS, 5 BOOKS, 10 BOOKS, **OR MORE TODAY,**
AND BECOME A LIFE CHANGER!

Thank you,

Don Nori Sr., Founder
Destiny Image
Since 1982

Unless

Carol Shields is the author of ten novels and three collections of short stories. *The Stone Diaries* won the Pulitzer Prize and was shortlisted for the Booker Prize. *Larry's Party* won the Orange Prize. Born and brought up in Chicago, Carol Shields has lived in Canada since 1957.

For more information on Carol Shields' *Unless* and to download a reading guide, visit www.4thestate.com/carolshields

THE WORK OF CAROL SHIELDS

POETRY
Others
Intersect
Coming to Canada

NOVELS
Larry's Party
The Stone Diaries
The Republic of Love
A Celibate Season (with Blanche Howard)
Mary Swann
A Fairly Conventional Woman
Happenstance
The Box Garden
Small Ceremonies

STORY COLLECTIONS
Dressing Up for the Carnival
The Orange Fish
Various Miracles

PLAYS
Departures and Arrivals
Thirteen Hands
Fashion, Power, Guilt and the Charity of Families (with Catherine Shields)
Anniversary (with David Williamson)

CRITICISM
Susanna Moodie: Voice and Vision

ANTHOLOGY
Dropped Threads: What We Aren't Told (Edited with Marjorie Anderson)
Dropped Threads 2: More of What We Aren't Told
(Edited with Marjorie Anderson)

BIOGRAPHY
Jane Austen: A Penguin Lives Biography